Cultivating Learning Communities of Belonging

Cultivating Learning Communities of Belonging

Practices for Inclusive Education

Edith H. van der Boom

Foreword by David I. Smith

CASCADE *Books* • Eugene, Oregon

CULTIVATING LEARNING COMMUNITIES OF BELONGING
Practices for Inclusive Education

Copyright © 2026 Edith H. van der Boom. All rights reserved. Except for brief quotations in critical publications or reviews, no part of this book may be reproduced in any manner without prior written permission from the publisher. Write: Permissions, Wipf and Stock Publishers, 199 W. 8th Ave., Suite 3, Eugene, OR 97401.

Cascade Books
An Imprint of Wipf and Stock Publishers
199 W. 8th Ave., Suite 3
Eugene, OR 97401

www.wipfandstock.com

PAPERBACK ISBN: 979-8-3852-5007-3
HARDCOVER ISBN: 979-8-3852-5008-0
EBOOK ISBN: 979-8-3852-5009-7

Cataloguing-in-Publication data:

Names: van der Boom, Edith H., author. | Smith, David I., foreword.

Title: Cultivating learning communities of belonging : practices for inclusive education / Edith H. van der Boom ; foreword by David I. Smith.

Description: Eugene, OR : Cascade Books, 2026 | Includes bibliographical references.

Identifiers: ISBN 979-8-3852-5007-3 (paperback) | ISBN 979-8-3852-5008-0 (hardcover) | ISBN 979-8-3852-5009-7 (ebook)

Subjects: LCSH: Inclusive education. | Teaching—Religious aspects—Christianity. | Education (Christian theology). | Christian education—Teaching methods.

Classification: BV4596.T43 .V36 2026 (paperback) | BV4596.T43 (ebook)

01/29/26

For my grandchildren—Noah, Riley, and Leah.
May you grow and flourish
in learning communities
where you are
known, valued, and belong.

For as in one body we have many members and not all the members have the same function, so we, who are many, are one body in Christ, and individually we are members one of another.

—Romans 12:5

Contents

Permissions | ix

Foreword by David I. Smith | xi

Acknowledgments | xv

Introduction | xvii

1 Cultivating School Culture | 1
2 Racial Justice | 14
3 School as a Place of Healing and Hope for Students Impacted by Trauma | 31
4 Communities Where Sexual Minority Youth Are Seen and Heard | 50
5 Indigenous Perspective Within Education | 62
6 Restorative Practices in Education | 84
7 Pedagogy and Community | 103
8 Cultivating a Community of Learners | 119
9 Hospitable Classrooms | 132

Bibliography | 143

Permissions

Scripture quotations are from the New Revised Standard Version Bible, copyright © 1989 National Council of the Churches of Christ in the United States of America. Used by permission. All rights reserved worldwide.

Portions of this work previously appeared as blog posts: "Kintsugi: Putting Broken Pieces Together" and "Ubuntu: I Am Because We Are." These materials are used with permission of Christian Deeper Learning and Christian Schools International.

"Kintsugi: Putting Broken Pieces Together." Christian Deeper Learning, May 24, 2022. https://www.christiandeeperlearning.org/post/kintsugi-putting-broken-pieces-together.

"Ubuntu: I Am Because We Are." Christian Deeper Learning, April 17, 2022. https://www.christiandeeperlearning.org/post/ubuntu-i-am-because-we-are.

Chapter 5: "Indigenous Perspective Within Education" was published in the *International Journal of Christianity and Education*, September 2, 2025.

Foreword

PROTECTING ONE ANOTHER

QUESTION AND ANSWER 107 seem to me to be the funniest part of the Heidelberg Catechism, a document not typically recognized for its humor.[1] The Heidelberg Catechism is a Reformed catechism published in 1653 as a teaching tool and still recognized as a doctrinal standard in many Reformed churches. It contains 129 questions and answers covering basic Christian doctrine and responsibilities, and question 107, following on from discussion of the biblical commandment against murder, goes like this:

> Is it enough then
> that we do not murder our neighbor
> in any such way?

One wonders whether this was a live question in the churches of the Reformation. "Pastor, you talk about a lot of things, but would it be enough if we could just avoid murdering each other? That would amount to success, right?" It seems like a low bar, until we recall how far our society falls short on even this basic norm. Perhaps it's not such a foolish question after all. The initial answer is impeccably concise and unambiguous:

> No.

---

1. I quote from Faith Alive Christian Resources, *Ecumenical Creeds and Reformed Confessions*, 63.

It seems we have to think a little further than avoiding bloodshed if we want to know how to treat those around us. The answer continues with a few more pointers:

> *By condemning envy, hatred, and anger*
> *God wants us*
> *to love our neighbors as ourselves,*
> *to be patient, peace-loving, gentle,*
> *merciful, and friendly toward them,*
> *to protect them from harm as much as we can,*
> *and to do good even to our enemies.*

The phrase that has stood out to me recently is the one that names the requirement to protect our neighbors from harm as much as we can. It's an important phrase. It resists resting content with the idea that we don't mean anyone any harm, that we have generally benign feelings toward the humans around us, that we are nice people and far be it from us to hurt anyone. It resists talking about love of neighbor as if the phrase just referred to an intention, a state of mind, or a sense of ourselves as kindly, agreeable people. It even pushes us a little beyond the idea of doing good, mentioned in the next line, because we can do at least a few good things without taking very much trouble to find out what is harming others. It assigns to us, as a direct consequence of Christian belief, the responsibility to actively protect others from harm "as much as we can."

Of course, the qualifying clause is important. There are bad things that will happen to our neighbors that we could not have prevented. In such cases our responsibilities turn toward compassion, mercy, lament, and service. But there is something to consider before the bad thing happens. Loving our neighbor also entails protection, helping to avoid the harm that threatens. Sometimes this does lie within our power.

It does not take much reflection to find the connection to the work of schooling. As many of us can testify, students, who are our neighbors, suffer harms in schools. There are catastrophic harms, since modern North American schools have so frequently become places where we do literally murder one another. There are interpersonal harms, such as bullying, assault, theft, or ridicule. There are systemic harms, such as mis-diagnosis of learning needs, poor, indifferent, or hostile teaching, or lack of access to needed educational services. There are subtle harms, tied to the complex ways in which a learner's sense of self and of their worth and possibilities are impacted by verbal messages, visual environments, curricular narratives, and teaching choices. Schools are places of enormous potential for the good; they give us a great deal that we need. They are also places where we experience harm. Not all of this is within our control. But some of it is.

If there were a convenient way to eliminate the possibility of harm occurring in schools we would have found it by now. Schools are all too human, partaking of our failings, prejudices, and hostilities as well as our hopes and service to our communities. Failure is at some level baked in, and all of our well-meant programs fall short of what could be. Yet being an educator, particularly an educator who is a Christian and accountable to the command to love our neighbor, entails commitment to protect others from harm as much as we can.

That involves more than being nice. Our students differ in their experience of culture, ethnicity, sexuality, ability, social location, and more. Navigating our differences well requires more than good intentions, especially when we are trying to maximize learning in their midst. Some knowledge, planning, and skill are needed. How might we build a community committed to protecting one another from harm amid differences? How would we commit to doing so "as much as we can"?

It does not seem a stretch to suggest that "as much as we can" might include a willingness to question and reexamine our current practices. It might include seeking out tools, such as a short book offering discussion, activity resources, and reflection questions. A book like this one, for instance. It might involve reading it alongside colleagues and actively discussing what to do about the bits that seem helpful. It might involve reading it less in the mode of whether it is the final word on everything and more in the mode of "Can I find something that helps?" It might involve taking one thing from it and starting a small process of change in your own classroom. Beginning is as simple as turning the page.

David I. Smith

Acknowledgments

THIS BOOK WAS BORN out of a course I teach at the Institute for Christian Studies titled Cultivating Learning Communities of Belonging. I'm deeply grateful to the students who participated in this course and pushed my thinking about what it truly means to foster belonging in schools and classrooms.

While the book explores key concepts related to belonging, it gains depth and meaning through the stories of educators who have brought these ideas into their own practice. Thank you to Carla Alblas, Heidi Blokland, Angie Bonvanie, Amanda Broadway, and Pauline Naftel for generously sharing your experiences and allowing me to include your stories.

I am deeply grateful to the many Christian educators who, despite their full schedules, took time to read a chapter—or even the entire manuscript—and provide thoughtful feedback. I owe thanks to David I. Smith for both his insightful feedback and his willingness to write the foreword for this book. I am also thankful to Brooklyn Sinclair and Owen Webb for their contributions.

A special thank you to my husband, Carl van der Boom, for reading the manuscript with care and offering valuable insights. Your love, encouragement, and support—through this project and beyond—are a gift I treasure deeply.

Introduction

> If identity and integrity are more fundamental to good teaching than technique—and if we want to grow as teachers—we must do something alien to academic culture: we must talk to each other about our inner lives—risky stuff in a profession that fears the personal and seeks safety in the technical, the distant, the abstract.
>
> —Parker Palmer

As a young student, I encountered numerous challenges in my learning journey and struggled to meet grade-level expectations—possibly due to a learning disability. Over time, I began to catch up academically, but the difficulties I faced as a student deeply shaped my path. These experiences inspired me to pursue a career in special education, driven by a desire to make learning a more supportive and empowering experience for students who, like me, struggled to thrive in a traditional school setting.

Cultivating Learning Communities of Belonging is a book for educators as they consider classroom and school cultures. Traditionally, teachers are trained to consider students' academic readiness levels, interests, and learning preferences; however, it is equally important to pay attention to social and cultural backgrounds, race, Indigenous perspectives, gender, human sexuality, and the like, as these topics impact and form school and classroom cultures.

INTRODUCTION

This book encourages educators to consider how students are different and how to create learning communities in which all students know that they belong. The driving question asked in this book is, "How can we create an inclusive community that values diversity?" In addition, this book seeks to help educators find clarity in answers to the following questions:

- What is the relationship between the daily behavior of educational leaders and the culture of their school?
- How do we awaken our students' knowledge, creativity, and critical reflective capacities?
- How do racism and other forms of oppression underlie achievement gaps and alienation within our schools?
- How can classroom learning be linked to larger movements seeking to effect change in the community?
- How can school culture be a vehicle for social change?
- How do we cultivate learning communities of belonging in our schools?

BEARING WITNESS TO EACH OTHER'S STORIES

One of the displays in the Human Rights Museum in Winnipeg, Manitoba, Canada, is the Witness Blanket. Carey Newman and several others created this blanket by gathering remnants from all of the residential schools across Canada. The blanket's purpose is to bear witness to the horrors of residential schooling. It bears witness to the losses and to the courage of Indigenous children who were taken from their homes and suffered from loneliness as well as both physical and emotional abuse. In the oral traditions of Indigenous peoples, a witness has an important role. To ensure nothing is forgotten, a witness observes, listens, and then remembers and shares what they have learned with others.[2]

2. Newman, "Welcome to the Witness Blanket," 2:52.

INTRODUCTION

Stories are one of the most meaningful ways that we blend knowledge and ideas. Psychologist Jerome Bruner suggests that storytelling is how we humans make sense of the world and shape our identities.[3] "Witnessing" involves more than just passively hearing someone speak. It is an active and engaged process that encompasses active listening, empathy, a nonjudgmental attitude, a reflective response, and validation of the speaker's experiences and emotions. By integrating these elements, witnessing becomes a deeply interactive process that fosters meaningful communication and understanding between individuals.[4]

To what do you bear witness? What is your story? After each chapter, I will include questions to consider. I hope that each reader of this book will be able to find conversation partners who will bear witness to one another and share their stories. Throughout the book, I have shared some of my stories. Sharing your stories will be the most meaningful way to integrate the ideas shared in this book and make them deeply contextualized for your teaching practice.

CULTIVATING AN INCLUSION MINDSET

In her book *Inclusion on Purpose: An Intersectional Approach to Creating a Culture of Belonging at Work*, Ruchika Tulshyan uses the "acronym BRIDGE as an approach to cultivating an inclusion mindset.

1. *Be* uncomfortable
2. *Reflect* (on what you don't know)
3. *Invite* feedback
4. *Defensiveness* doesn't help
5. *Grow* from your mistakes
6. *Expect* that change takes time."[5]

   3. Bruner, *Acts of Meaning*.
   4. Lepp-Kaethler and Rust-Akinbolaji, "Welcoming the Guest."
   5. Tulshyan, *Inclusion on Purpose*, 42.

INTRODUCTION

The work of creating a culture of belonging is going to be uncomfortable. I hope that sitting in the discomfort of injustice will lead to the transformation of both ourselves and the world.

If we want people to fully engage and bring their whole, authentic selves—to innovate, solve problems, and serve others, we must be vigilant in creating a culture where people feel safe, seen, heard, and respected.[6] The phrase "everyone is welcome at the table" is a common one that demonstrates a community of belonging. However, "making room at a table" does not guarantee that one will belong. If a table is surrounded by people who share similar characteristics, they feel safe to be their full selves. In contrast, people who do not share these characteristics become a minority to the rest of the table. True belonging is when everyone builds that table together in a way that reflects each person's unique gifts, and each person's contributions are welcomed and valued.

HOW TO USE THIS BOOK

Although one may read this book independently, it is structured as a study guide for groups of educators or staff teams. The process involves each participant reading the agreed-upon chapter, followed by a designated time to meet together. After each chapter, I suggest incorporating restorative classroom practices, which I call "Together." These sections include what I refer to as *name, game,* and *frame*. I recommend that each of these three activities be experienced collectively as a large group before engaging in small group discussions about the chapter and, more importantly, sharing personal stories. These practices serve as ways for the group to build a learning community of belonging among themselves. Some may also be appropriate for teachers to try with their students. Here's a brief overview of these practices:

1. *Name*: Start by having each participant share their name (especially when there are new staff members present) and/or a

---

6. Brown, *Dare to Lead*.

brief personal or professional update. This helps in building a sense of community and trust within the group.
2. *Game*: Engage in a short, interactive activity or game that fosters connection and eases participants into the session. This might be a team-building exercise, or a simple icebreaker designed to promote a positive and relaxed atmosphere. The goal is to build a community of belonging.
3. *Frame*: Set the context for the discussion by summarizing key themes or questions from the chapter. This framing helps participants focus on the main ideas and prepares them for deeper conversation.

By incorporating these practices, groups can create a supportive and engaging environment that encourages meaningful dialogue and personal sharing. In this way, I hope teachers will not only learn about cultivating learning communities of belonging but also experience it as well.

At the end of each chapter, I have included several questions designed to serve as conversation starters. To structure the discussion effectively, I suggest small group (ideally groups of three) discussions that encourage participants to share stories. This is then followed by a whole group debrief.

Choose which months you plan to meet. September, December, and June are often very busy times of year when you may not have the capacity to meet. See table 1 for a sample outline.

INTRODUCTION

Table 1

Sample Book Study Structure

Month	Chapter	Time
August	Introduction and Chapter 1: Cultivating School Culture	75 minutes
September	Chapter 2: Racial Justice	75 minutes
October	Chapter 3: School as a Place of Healing and Hope for Students Impacted by Trauma	75 minutes
November	Chapter 4: Communities Where Sexual Minority Youth Are Seen and Heard	75 minutes
January	Chapter 5: Indigenous Perspective Within Education	75 minutes
February	Chapter 6: Restorative Practices in Education	75 minutes
March	Chapter 7: Pedagogy and Community	75 minutes
April	Chapter 8: Cultivating a Community of Learners	75 minutes
May	Chapter 9: Hospitable Classrooms	75 minutes

Note. This sample book study does not meet in December or June.

Consider setting aside about 60 to 75 minutes per month for each chapter. I suggest 15 to 20 minutes for the name, game, and frame, 30 minutes for small group discussion, and 15 to 25 minutes to wrap up as a whole group. By following this structure, the sessions will promote active engagement, foster deeper connections among participants, and enhance the overall learning experience.

1

Cultivating School Culture

The most important thing each of us can know is our unique gift and how to use it in the world. Individuality is cherished and nurtured, because, in order for the whole to flourish, each of us has to be strong in who we are and carry our gifts with conviction, so they can be shared with others.

—Robin Wall Kimmerer

THE THREE SISTERS

FOR MANY YEARS, INDIGENOUS people have planted their gardens in a style they refer to as the Three Sisters.[1] The Three Sisters, consisting of corn, beans, and squash, feed the people and our imaginations of how we might live together. Together, they are planted in the same patch of soil each spring. Colonists thought Indigenous peoples did not know how to farm when they first saw their gardens. In their minds, each species needed to be planted individually in a straight row, not in a three-dimensional

---

1. Kimmerer, *Braiding Sweetgrass*, 129.

sprawl. However, the gardens of Indigenous peoples were abundant with food.

After the Three Sisters are planted, the corn is the first to shoot up through the soil. It takes on the water in the soil, triggering the growth of the corn embryo within the seed, and then appears as a slender white spike that greens quickly in the sunlight. The leaves unfurl one by one, and the corn stands alone until the others are ready. The bean seed swells as it drinks in the soil water and then bursts open, sending a rootling down into the ground. Only after the root is secure does the stem make its way above ground. The bean can take its time finding the light as its first leaves are already packaged in the seed. By the time it breaks through the surface of the soil, the corn may already be fifteen centimeters tall. The squash takes its time. It may be weeks before the leaves split the seams of the seed coat and break free. Each plant has its own pace. The sequence of its germination is an important part of the relationship they have with each other and the success of an abundant crop.

The corn is the firstborn. Its highest priority at the beginning is to grow a strong, tall stem quickly. It needs to be there for the second sister, the bean. While the corn focuses on height, the bean focuses on leaf growth. When the corn is about knee high, the bean changes its focus from making leaves to extending itself into a long vine. This slender green string wanders into the air, looking for something to support it—like a corn stem. The vine wraps itself around the corn in a graceful upward spiral. If the corn had not started early, the bean plant could have strangled it, but if the timing is right, then the corn can easily support it. The squash has taken its time to bloom in a way that seems thoughtful and wise. It grows outward, extending along the ground away from the corn and bean plants. It develops large, broad leaves that shelter the soil at the base of the corn and beans so that moisture stays in and weeds stay out.

RECIPROCITY

The story of the Three Sisters teaches us about reciprocity. Each plant has a mutual dependence on one another. The corn stands over two meters tall. Each green leaf curls away from the stem, not one over the other, so that each one can gather light. The bean twines itself between the leaves of the corn stalk so that it does not interfere with its work. In places where there are no corn leaves, the bean develops both leaves and clusters of flowers that will later grow into a bean pod. Without the support of the corn, the beans would grow in a tangle on the ground, thus being vulnerable to predators. The leaves of the squash use the light that makes its way past both the corn and bean leaves so that none goes to waste.

Above ground, one can see how the sisters' leaves respect each other's space. The same is true underground when one looks at their roots. The corn has a shallow network of fine and fibrous roots that do not go very deep. It receives the first of the water from incoming rain. The taproots of the bean plant are deeper and so they drink up the rainwater after the corn has finished. The roots of the squash move away from the others. Whenever the stem of the squash touches the ground, it puts down roots far from that of the corn and bean roots. They share the soil in a similar way in which they share the sunlight so that there is enough for everyone.

At first glance, it may seem that the bean is solely a benefactor, but the rules or reciprocity require that none can take more than they give. The corn ensures that there is light available, and the leaves of the squash reduce weeds and conserve the moisture in the soil. To see the gift of the bean, one must look underground. There is one thing that each of the Three Sisters needs, and yet it is often in short supply—nitrogen. Nitrogen is a nutrient that is necessary for the growth of plants. Although it is in abundant supply in the atmosphere, it cannot be used by plants in this form. As it turns out, beans take nitrogen from the atmosphere and transform it into a usable nutrient, together with the help of a bacteria called Rhizobium. With the bean root as a host, it grows an oxygen-free nodule to house the bacterium which in turn shares nitrogen with the plant. Together they create a nitrogen fertilizer that enters the soil which can then be used by the corn and squash. The layers of reciprocity in this garden are abounding as we see relationships between the corn, bean, and squash, as well as between the bean and the bacteria, and, ultimately, with people who plant, weed, water, and enjoy the harvest.[2]

Together, these Three Sisters respect and support each other, using their gifts and receiving the gifts of others. They cooperate rather than compete with each other. At the end of the summer, the ears of corn angle out from the stalk, the beans hang in heavy clusters, and the squash swell at one's feet. The Three Sisters' garden produces more food than if each plant grew alone. It is impressive to see how each of the Three Sisters works together. Each plant acts to promote its own growth. Interestingly, when individual plants thrive, the entire ecosystem flourishes.[3]

DIVERSITY

There are lessons that the Three Sisters teach us about diversity and reciprocity that can strengthen our schools and classrooms. The Three Sisters teach us the importance of how our differences can be used to support one another, how timing is essential, and how, in order for us to flourish together, we need to support each individual so that each one's gifts can be strengthened and thereby benefit the whole.

Our staff relationships and our leadership team model for students what we desire to see lived out in the classroom. Some educators choose to work alone rather than together with their colleagues, as it seems that doing things independently is easier than trying to work with others. Collaboration is an important part of both school leadership and teaching. In terms of school leadership, the school principal does well to surround herself with others in the school who take on responsibilities within the

---

2. Kimmerer, *Braiding Sweetgrass*, 129–34.
3. Kimmerer, *Braiding Sweetgrass*, 134.

context of pedagogy. This may include vice-principals or instructional leaders. Instructional leaders (sometimes given the title of lead teacher) play a significant role in creating a strong learning environment as they focus on pedagogy, curriculum, and, most importantly, individual students' needs.

EQUITY

For most of my years as an elementary and secondary student, I attended Christian schools. I trusted that my teachers had my best interests in mind. As an adult I now look back on those experiences and wonder how invested some of my teachers actually were in who I was as a student. I have recently read some of the report cards I was given as a child and quickly noted the difference in comments from one teacher to the next. In grade five, my homeroom teacher commented on my December report, "Edith is generally willing to work, but she doesn't put quite enough effort into it. I believe she is capable of better work than she has done this term. Somehow, she does not seem at home in grade five. 31 times this term, she has reported that her assignments were not done. She gets behind, especially in spelling, reading, and math." Another teacher who taught me science, art, and music wrote, "Edith works hard to keep up with her work, but she still finds it difficult. Regular review of her [science] notes should be encouraged. Edith has a good sense of beauty in art. She works diligently and neatly." What different perspectives each of these teachers had of me. Indeed, I did not feel at home in my fifth grade class, especially with my homeroom teacher. The teacher who taught me science, music, and art knew more about me, and as a student, I was able to work more effectively with her.

Students may struggle in school for many different reasons. Structural inequalities can lead to psychological inequalities, which in turn can reinforce the effects of structural inequalities on achievement and future opportunities.[4] Although Christian

---

4. Claro et al., "Growth Mindset Tempers the Effects of Poverty on Academic Achievement," 8667.

schools may genuinely aim to serve all students, many students from diverse backgrounds often feel voiceless and are not given the opportunity to envision and shape their school communities.[5] A key barrier to inclusion is the *essentializing* of culture—treating cultural groups as fixed, uniform, and unchanging, and assuming that all students within a group identify in the same way.[6] As educators, we must move beyond equality, where everything is the same for everyone, and work toward equity, recognizing that we do not all start from the same place and seeking to create spaces of true belonging for all.

INCLUSION

Having begun my career in special education, I was passionate about creating inclusive learning spaces that intentionally cared for students according to their learning preferences, readiness levels, and physical needs. However, I was not well versed in inclusion that considered different social and cultural contexts, racial justice, Indigenous perspectives, or human sexuality. My experiences have inspired me to deepen my understanding and to advocate for more holistic forms of inclusion.

A school should be a learning community characterized by close, informal relationships where individual circumstances matter, acceptance is unconditional, and cooperation and collegiality thrive. Leadership should be shared, self-sacrifice for the benefit of others should be common, and all members should work hard to center their beliefs, values, and understandings, for this is a community in which everyone is an active crew member on a shared journey, and no one is merely a passenger.[7]

Diversity, equity, and inclusion are each unique principles, but all three are needed to cultivate a healthy school culture.[8]

---

5. Chen et al., "From White to Mosaic," 67.

6. Sleeter, "Confronting the Marginalization of Culturally Responsive Pedagogy," 570.

7. Hekman, "Schools as Communities of Grace," para. 5.

8. Tisby, *How to Fight Racism*, 121.

Diversity focuses on who is present, equity decides who has access to the resources in a community, and inclusion determines who is welcome and feels that they belong.[9] All three are essential to creating learning communities of belonging.

TOGETHER

Name

Gather in a circle. Begin by welcoming all participants with a greeting of your choice (e.g., hi, bonjour, good day, good morning, etc.) and your name (e.g., Hello, my name is Edith). Ask all participants to respond with the same greeting and the person's name (e.g., Hello, Edith). Repeat this for each participant. Although many staff members may already know each other, sharing each other's names is helpful for new staff members. If there are no new staff members, you may consider skipping this greeting.

After everyone has been greeted, go around the circle once more by having each person answer the following question: "What is one thing you enjoy doing that most people don't know about?" If you have a large group, you may want to ask everyone to limit their response to one or two sentences.

Game

Identity mapping is an excellent way to foster understanding and empathy among participants by encouraging them to explore and share both their visible and invisible identities.[10] Here's a step-by-step guide to implementing this exercise:

1. *Introduction.* Briefly introduce the concept of social identities, explaining the difference between visible and invisible identities. Emphasize the importance of understanding both

---

9. Tisby, *How to Fight Racism*, 121.
10. Tulshyan, *Inclusion on Purpose*, 69–71.

aspects to build a more inclusive and empathetic workplace or community.

2. *Drawing the Identity Map.* Ask each participant to draw a large circle and a large square next to each other on a piece of paper. Instruct them to write their visible identities in the circle. These might include attributes like gender, age, race, hair color, etc. In the square, have them write their invisible identities. These can include roles, personal traits, hobbies, beliefs, etc.

3. *Examples.* Provide your own examples to help participants understand the task. In the circle, I usually write my visible identities as:

- Female
- White
- Middle-aged
- Blue eyes
- Blonde/Grey hair

In the square, I write my invisible identities as:

- Mother and grandmother
- Daughter of Dutch immigrants
- Introvert
- Swimmer
- Social justice–minded

4. *Pairing Up.* Ask participants to pair up with someone who seems similar to them based on visible identities. This could be someone of the same race, gender, or nationality. Then, have them share their identity maps and discuss identities and the experiences they have had because of them.

5. *Switching Partners.* Now, ask participants to find a partner who appears to be quite different from them in terms of

visible identities. Again, have them share their identity maps and discuss their experiences and identities.

6. *Reflection.* Bring the group back together for a debriefing session. Encourage participants to reflect on and discuss the following questions:

    - How did it feel to share your identity with someone similar to you?
    - How did it feel to share your identity with someone different from you?
    - What surprised you about the conversations?
    - Did you discover any unexpected commonalities or differences?

This identity mapping exercise can be a powerful tool for enhancing mutual understanding and fostering a more inclusive environment. By exploring both visible and invisible identities, participants can gain a deeper appreciation of the richness and complexity of the people around them.

Frame

Ask participants to read 1 Cor 12:12–27 independently and underline the parts that are most significant to them. After everyone has read it silently to themselves, read it out loud. Have each participant simultaneously read out only the sections they have underlined.

One Body with Many Members

> [12] For just as the body is one and has many members, and all the members of the body, though many, are one body, so it is with Christ. [13] For in the one Spirit we were all baptized into one body—Jews or Greeks, slaves or free—and we were all made to drink of one Spirit.

[14] Indeed, the body does not consist of one member but of many. [15] If the foot would say, "Because I am not a hand, I do not belong to the body," that would not make it any less a part of the body. [16] And if the ear would say, "Because I am not an eye, I do not belong to the body," that would not make it any less a part of the body. [17] If the whole body were an eye, where would the hearing be? If the whole body were hearing, where would the sense of smell be? [18] But as it is, God arranged the members in the body, each one of them, as he chose. [19] If all were a single member, where would the body be? [20] As it is, there are many members yet one body. [21] The eye cannot say to the hand, "I have no need of you," nor again the head to the feet, "I have no need of you." [22] On the contrary, the members of the body that seem to be weaker are indispensable, [23] and those members of the body that we think less honorable we clothe with greater honor, and our less respectable members are treated with greater respect, [24] whereas our more respectable members do not need this. But God has so arranged the body, giving the greater honor to the inferior member, [5] that there may be no dissension within the body, but the members may have the same care for one another. [26] If one member suffers, all suffer together with it; if one member is honored, all rejoice together with it.
[27] Now you are the body of Christ and individually members of it.[11]

Prayer

Open in a prayer to ask God to bless your conversations together:

Creator God,
    Thank you for the gift of gathering in community. We are grateful for the calling you have placed on our lives to teach. As we reflect on our practices, guide us in discovering what it means to teach faithfully in our present context. Help us to see how our faith

11. 1 Cor 12:12–27.

and imagination can work hand in hand to bring grace and truth into the lives of our students and our school community.

We recognize that teaching is more than passing on knowledge—it is a sacred role in shaping students as your image-bearers. May our conversation today be rich with insight and purpose. Show us clearly how we might join in your ongoing work of restoration.

In Jesus's name we pray,
Amen.

GUIDING QUESTIONS

- Break into small groups of three and ask one person in each group to guide the conversation.
- Take turns sharing one quote from the chapter that stood out to you. Explain why it resonated with you personally or professionally.
- Use the questions provided below as conversation prompts. There is no need to answer every question—let them serve as starting points to spark meaningful discussion.
- After the discussion time ends, come back together as a full group. Invite each small group to share one key insight or meaningful moment from their conversation.

Diversity

1. How do the Three Sisters illustrate the value of diversity in their interdependence and growth?
2. How can we apply the lessons from the Three Sisters' relationship to foster diversity in classrooms or workplaces?
3. What are the challenges individuals or institutions face when trying to move from a monoculture mindset to one that embraces diversity?

Equity

4. The story highlights the unique timing and roles of the Three Sisters. How can this idea help us rethink equity in education or leadership?
5. How does the principle of equity differ from equality, and why is equity more effective in fostering true belonging?
6. Reflecting on Edith's personal school experiences, how can teachers ensure they recognize and nurture the strengths of all students?

Inclusion

7. What role does inclusion play in ensuring that diversity and equity lead to a flourishing community?
8. How can educators and leaders avoid essentializing culture and instead promote an inclusive environment?
9. What are specific ways schools can address structural inequalities that lead to psychological barriers for students from diverse backgrounds?

Reciprocity

10. What does reciprocity look like in a school community, and how can it strengthen relationships among staff and students?
11. The Three Sisters demonstrate giving and receiving among plants. How can individuals balance giving and receiving in collaborative environments?

Personal Reflection

12. How does your unique "gift" contribute to your community, and how do you ensure it aligns with the needs of the whole?
13. Reflect on a time when you felt truly included in a community. What factors contributed to that sense of belonging?
14. What steps can leaders take to create communities where everyone feels valued and heard?

2

Racial Justice

> But racism is more than an individual or interpersonal attitude. It includes systems, structures, and institutions owned and operated by those who hold the power to make decisions.
> —Jemar Tisby

MY RACIAL IDENTITY

BOTH OF MY PARENTS left the Netherlands as single young adults and came to Canada for more opportunities. For my mom, that meant working as a bank teller and becoming self-sufficient. For my dad, it meant moving in with an older brother and his sister-in-law when he arrived in Canada. He was able to get a job doing landscaping. Shortly after they met, they married and decided to begin their own business. At first it was textiles and floor covering. My mom would sew the drapes, and my dad would install carpet. Later they just sold floor covering and hired others to install it.

My parents' stories of immigration play a significant role in my own racial identity. I grew up hearing about how little they had when they started their life in Canada, how they worked hard, and how God blessed us as a family. Our home was one in which there were reminders of the country in which my parents had come from. This included Delft blue pottery, decorative wooden shoes, but more significantly Dutch foods such as Gouda and Edam cheese, croquettes, chocolate letters which were gifted at Christmas, *oliebollen* (technically translated as oil balls but taste like deep fried donuts) on New Year's Eve, and candy such as peppermints and *droppies* (salty black licorice) which we were given during church each Sunday. My parents decided not to be intentional about sharing the Dutch language with me and my siblings. They spoke English to us at home and only used Dutch when they did not want us to know what they were talking about. Since we were living in Canada, they felt we should speak English. I regret that this was what they decided, as I would have loved to be multilingual, like so many people around the world.

Everyone in my world was white. Whiteness was what was "normal" in my world. My school and church community were, for the most part, made up of other Dutch immigrant families throughout my K-12 years. One of the few experiences in which I had exposure to a different culture was my grade-school friend, who was also white, and whose parents immigrated from Ireland. Even when I went to university, I was surrounded by others who were immigrants with white parents. It was not until I was well into adulthood that I started to be aware of how racial identities mattered. I have experienced over fifty years of what Stephen Brookfield calls "ideological conditioning into white supremacy."[1]

KNOWING OURSELVES AS INSTRUCTORS

Racial privilege has and continues to shape the experiences of educators from dominant cultures and is an ongoing journey of de-centering. Reflecting on one's racial identity is an important part of understanding another's racial identity. I am aware that the way I learn and participate in racial and/or cultural identity is very

---

1. Brookfield, *Becoming a Critically Reflective Teacher*, 214.

specific to my own experience, and yet, as a woman with white skin, this is something that I have done very little of. Considering one's racial identity, however, is a regular practice for those of color.[2] Racism functions at multiple levels—individual, group, and institutional. Although I am not intentionally racist, I am advantaged in inherently racist systems. There are things that I have done or have been a part of that have been racist, and I belong to a race that for much of history represents the oppressors. As a teacher, I have been in classrooms where whiteness has been made to be the standard by using only dolls, toys, and books in which white children are represented, and where Band-Aids are used that only match white skin. Whether intentional or unintentional, conscious or unconscious, racism is still racism.

Recently a friend shared with me a hurtful experience that her son had when he was in high school. A teacher came up to him and asked him where he was from. When he informed this teacher that he was from a neighboring town the teacher asked again, "No, where are you from?" Because the student was of Asian descent, this teacher assumed that the student must have come from a different country. The fact, however, was that this student, with Asian features, was born and raised in Canada. Although the question asked by the teacher was not meant to be hurtful or racist—it was. Without having built a relationship with the student or provided a safe environment, the seemingly innocent question created a hurtful and racist interaction.

Becoming aware of the way we learn and participate in a racial and/or cultural identity is important and challenging.[3] For instructors in the dominant culture, confronting the evidence of racial privilege found in course and curricular development can be especially humbling.[4] Racism can be understood as a systemic structure of racialized advantage that operates across individual, institutional, and cultural levels. Confronting its influence involves

2. Tisby, *How to Fight Racism*.
3. Chen et al., "From White to Mosaic," 69; Tisby, *How to Fight Racism*, 185–86.
4. Ramsay, "Teaching Effectively," 22.

an ongoing effort to recognize and unsettle the privileges that shape lived experience.[5]

KNOWING OUR STUDENTS

As our classrooms become more racially and culturally diverse, there is a greater chance of encountering students who do not belong to the dominant culture and, therefore, are more likely to experience the pain of racism.[6] Providing students with the opportunity to become familiar with each other's racial and cultural heritages, through speaking and listening, can be the start of creating a more inclusive and safe environment for brave conversations where all student voices are valued and respected. As educators who are challenging our practices of listening and speaking, it is important to provide space for students to share their own stories and to have a posture of openness when those who have experienced injury by current practices voice their pain. Together with our students, we need to consider ways in which we can support and foster these spaces for truth and reconciliation.

UNCOVERING UNCONSCIOUS BIAS

Teaching that affirms each student's identity and sense of belonging lays the foundation for an inclusive classroom. Such classrooms become spaces where educators and students together examine their roles in shaping communities rooted in justice and inclusivity. A key part of this shared journey involves open conversations about diverse racial and cultural heritages. As students learn about one another's backgrounds, they are better able to recognize their own assumptions and biases. This process of uncovering unconscious bias requires intentional time and space for listening to each other's stories and perspectives, fostering deeper understanding and mutual respect.

---

5. Ramsay, "Teaching Effectively," 20.
6. Chen et al., "From White to Mosaic," 67; Ramsay, "Teaching Effectively," 20.

One very practical way to begin critically reflecting on your teaching practice is to be aware of what resources are available in your classrooms. Books written by and representing different cultures are important in creating an inclusive classroom environment. Teaching Black history throughout the year and not only during Black History Month helps us hear a more complete story of what has happened in the past.

Stephen Brookfield recounts an experience in one of his leadership classes where he unintentionally excluded a student from a minority background.[7] He had asked everyone in the class to share their initial reflections on an issue, and after listening, he summarized the main themes that had surfaced. Only then did a white female student point out that one person had not been invited to speak—a young Asian American woman. Caught off guard, Brookfield apologized and gave her the opportunity to contribute.

During the break, he reflected on what had happened and recognized it as a clear instance of microaggression. Although he had not deliberately meant to leave anyone out, his actions nevertheless reinforced a pattern of exclusion. When class resumed, he acknowledged the oversight again and explained that this was a real-life example of how racial microaggressions often operate—subtle, unintended behaviors rooted in long-standing patterns of socialization and cultural dominance.

One white student dismissed his concern, suggesting he was overthinking a simple mistake. Brookfield clarified that microaggressions are not about intent but about the cumulative weight of behaviors shaped by systemic inequality. At that point, the overlooked student shared that similar experiences of being ignored had occurred in nearly every course she had taken at the university, underlining how persistent and damaging such patterns can be.

A critically reflective examination of culture, race, and ethnicity can help us better celebrate the differences of our students, coworkers, and community. Using the example of the situation in which a student was asked where they are from can help us

---

7. Brookfield, *Becoming a Critically Reflective Teacher*, 215–16.

critically reflect on our unconscious bias and on the racism that may be playing out in our classroom.

What? A student is asked where he is from because of his racial features.

So What? This student feels that this teacher was suggesting that he did not belong because he looked different than other students in his school.

Now What? Create safe spaces that invite students to be brave and tell their own stories of race and culture.

Using these prompts may help us become aware of our unconscious bias, encourage a safe space for brave conversations, and begin the work of truth and reconciliation. Our journey to creating both diverse and inclusive learning environments requires us to be critically reflective in our practice as we strive to create learning communities of belonging.

As I reflect on my practice as an educator, I recognize that much of my attention has been directed toward students' academic achievements as a way of fostering their sense of belonging. While this is valuable, I am increasingly aware of the need to understand my students more fully, particularly in relation to their racial and cultural contexts. Experiencing God's grace transforms how we see the world, shaping our vision with love and drawing us to care about what matters to God—to delight in what brings joy to God's heart and to lament what causes sorrow. This transformed way of seeing profoundly influences how we perceive people, cultures, and the world around us.[8] I hope that, through such a lens, we may truly see our students, nurturing their sense of belonging so that they may flourish as the people God has created them to be.

SEEING PAST PRIVILEGE

Racism can be defined as the belief that certain races, especially one's own, are inherently superior to others.[9] However, many

---

8. Mouw, *Abraham Kuyper*, 92.
9. Merriam-Webster, "Racism."

scholars recognize three united prongs of racism: prejudices, power structures, and societal norms.[10] This definition suggests that while a person may not believe that they are racially superior to others, they can still contribute to racism by being complicit with the present power structures, which are designed to protect power and privilege in specific geographical locations.[11]

Racism is indeed a complex set of values and beliefs that individuals learn and assimilate throughout their lives.[12] This ideology shapes a person's perspective on the world, influencing how they perceive and interact with others based on racial categorizations.[13] Seeing past privilege requires self-awareness, education, and proactive steps toward understanding and dismantling the systemic advantages some groups have over others.

Privilege can come in many forms, including race, gender, socioeconomic status, sexual orientation, and ability. We need to educate ourselves about different types of privileges and how they manifest in everyday life. Microaggressions are subtle, often unintentional, discriminatory comments or behaviors that can be offensive and harmful. For people of color, the racial microaggressions experienced over one's lifetime have been described as "death by a thousand cuts" and contribute to the harmful effect on one's well-being.[14]

Becoming anti-racist includes intentional steps toward changing learned behavior that has been learned through societal norms, media portrayals, familial attitudes, and peer influences that can perpetuate racial biases.

Andrew M. Ibrahim outlines a journey toward becoming anti-racist through three progressive zones.[15] He outlines steps to transition from a racist mindset to an anti-racist one. The journey begins with the *Fear Zone*, where we avoid confronting racism,

10. De La Torre, *Reading the Bible from the Margins*.
11. De La Torre, *Reading the Bible from the Margins*.
12. Brookfield, *Becoming a Critically Reflective Teacher*, 210.
13. Brookfield, *Becoming a Critically Reflective Teacher*, 210.
14. Kim, "How a Pad-Mounted Transformer."
15. Ibrahim, "Becoming Anti-Racist."

aiming instead to remain comfortable. Next is the *Learning Zone*, where we recognize racism as a serious issue and commit to learning about racism and systemic injustices. Finally, in the *Growth Zone*, we examine our own biases and actively speak out against racial injustice in all areas of our lives, including schools and classrooms. Progressing through these zones requires humility, as mistakes are inevitable along the way. Though challenging, the path to becoming anti-racist is essential.

As we strive to be part of God's story of redemption and renewal we continue to falter and need to return to Jesus for forgiveness. We are better at highlighting our good works than those things we have been a part of that are unjust. Let us honor others' stories, check our assumptions, and embrace discomfort.

BECOMING AN ANTI-RACIST

I encourage you to take some time to reflect on your own racial identity. Consider the following questions:

- How has your racial identity influenced your life experiences?
- What messages did you receive about different races growing up?
- How do your racial experiences differ from those of people from other racial backgrounds?

Writing down your thoughts can be a powerful exercise. It allows you to confront uncomfortable truths, celebrate your heritage, and recognize the impact of race on your life and the lives of others.

Understanding one's racial identity is just the first step in becoming an anti-racist. Becoming an anti-racist requires deliberate actions and continuous self-reflection. Here are some steps to guide you on this journey:

1. *Educate Yourself:* Learn about the history and current realities of racism. Read books, attend workshops, and engage with diverse perspectives to deepen your understanding.

2. *Reflect on Privilege*: Recognize your own privileges and how they impact your interactions with others. This reflection is crucial for understanding how you can use your privilege to support marginalized communities.
3. *Speak Out*: Use your voice to challenge racist behaviors and policies. Whether in personal conversations or public forums, speaking out against racism is vital for creating change.
4. *Support Marginalized Communities*: Stand in solidarity with marginalized groups by supporting their causes, amplifying their voices, and being an ally in the fight for justice.
5. *Implement Anti-Racist Practices*: In your personal and professional life, strive to implement practices that promote equity and inclusion. This includes creating inclusive environments in schools and classrooms.

THE IMPORTANCE OF ANTI-RACIST PRACTICES IN SCHOOLS AND CLASSROOMS

Schools and classrooms are critical spaces for fostering anti-racist practices. As educators and students, we have the responsibility to create environments where all students feel valued and respected. Here are some reasons why anti-racist practices are essential in educational settings:

- *Promote Equity:* Anti-racist practices help address the systemic inequities that affect students of color. By promoting fair treatment and equal opportunities, we can ensure that all students have the chance to succeed.
- *Encourage Empathy and Understanding:* When students learn about different racial experiences and histories, they develop empathy and understanding for their peers. This understanding is crucial for building inclusive communities.
- *Prepare Students for a Diverse World:* Exposure to diverse perspectives and anti-racist teachings prepares students to

navigate and contribute positively to an increasingly diverse world.

- *Foster Critical Thinking:* Anti-racist education encourages students to think critically about societal structures and their roles within them. This critical thinking is essential for developing informed and active citizens.

Embracing our racial identities and committing to anti-racist practices are vital steps toward creating a more just and equitable society. By sharing our stories and taking deliberate actions, we can contribute to meaningful changes in our schools, communities, and beyond.

TOGETHER

Name

Gather in a circle. Share one memory related to your culture/race.

Game

The following activity requires participant vulnerability. I like to warn participants of this ahead of time. The purpose of this exercise is to encourage reflection on privilege and how certain groups benefit from it while others remain marginalized. This exercise, often referred to as a "privilege walk," offers both a physical and an intellectual understanding of how privilege affects individuals, often in an unconscious manner.[16]

The activity begins with participants standing in a straight line, holding hands, across a large open space. In silence, they step forward or backward based on their responses to statements about circumstances beyond their control. For example, one might ask, "Have you ever been told you couldn't do something because of your gender or race?" Such questions highlight how social and cultural dynamics, such as teachers assigning tasks based on gender,

16. Ramsay, "Teaching Effectively," 20.

influence opportunities from a young age. Over time, the straight line of participants will break as people step in different directions based on their experiences.

This exercise works best in a trusting environment with prior discussion and has consistently led to deeper understanding for both those who have lived privileged lives and those from marginalized racial or cultural groups.

Examples to use to explain the game:

- If you are right-handed, take one step forward.
- If your sex or race is widely represented in school leadership, take one step forward.
- If you have difficulty finding hair products, make-up for your skin complexion, or a hairstylist, take one step backward.

General Privilege Questions

1. If your parents went to college, take one step forward.
2. If you were raised in a two-parent household, take one step forward.
3. If you grew up in a home that you or your family owned, take one step forward.
4. If you have ever been told you can't do something because of your gender, take one step backward.
5. If you've ever been the only person of your race or ethnicity in a room, take one step backward.
6. If you've ever had to worry about your family's ability to pay bills, take one step backward.
7. If you can walk around your neighborhood without fear of being harassed, take one step forward.
8. If you were ever bullied or made fun of for something you couldn't change, take one step backward.

9. If you ever had to skip a meal or were hungry because there was not enough money to buy food, take one step backward.
10. If your parents were able to hire a tutor for you if you were struggling in school, take one step forward.

Racial or Cultural Privilege Questions

1. If you can easily find books and movies with characters who look like you, take one step forward.
2. If your racial or ethnic group is widely represented in history books and school curricula, take one step forward.
3. If you have never been followed or closely watched in a store because of your race, take one step forward.
4. If you've never been stopped or questioned by police because of your race, take one step forward.
5. If you have never been called a racial slur, take one step forward.

Gender Privilege Questions

1. If you've ever felt unsafe walking alone at night because of your gender, take one step backward.
2. If you've never had to worry about how to dress to avoid unwanted attention, take one step forward.
3. If people rarely interrupt or talk over you because of your gender, take one step forward.
4. If you've ever been paid less than others for the same work due to your gender, take one step backward.

Sexuality Privilege Questions

1. If you have never had to hide your sexuality for fear of discrimination or judgment, take one step forward.
2. If your family and friends have always accepted your sexual orientation, take one step forward.
3. If you've ever feared holding hands with your partner in public, take one step backward.

Socioeconomic Privilege Questions

1. If you've ever had to rely on public transportation because you didn't have access to a car, take one step backward.
2. If your family had health insurance throughout your childhood, take one step forward.
3. If you attended a private school or a school with abundant resources, take one step forward.
4. If you ever received free or reduced lunch at school, take one step backward.

Physical and Mental Health Privilege Questions

1. If you have never been discriminated against because of a physical or mental disability, take one step forward.
2. If you've ever had to miss out on an opportunity due to lack of accessibility (physical or otherwise), take one step backward.
3. If you've never had to worry about affording mental health care, take one step forward.
4. If you've ever been made fun of or treated differently because of a health issue, take one step backward.

After the exercise, it is important to have a conversation that allows participants to reflect on their experience and discuss what they have learned.

Reflection Questions

- What was the main goal of this activity?
- What insights did you gain from participating?
- Can you describe what happened during the exercise? Did anything catch you by surprise?
- How did it feel to be part of the group stepping forward or stepping back?
- What emotions did you experience being at the front or back of the room?
- Was there a moment when you wished to be part of the group moving forward?
- What lessons from this exercise can we apply to our everyday lives?
- How can the knowledge you've gained from this experience influence your work as an educator?

Frame

Video

Watch "Powerful Poetry About Racial Discrimination: Mandisa Volo's Winning Speech." Mandisa Volo, a grade seven student at Kamloops School of the Arts, took first place in the 2019 Rotary Grade 6/7 Speech Competition in Kamloops, BC.[17] She captivated the audience by starting and concluding with her original poetry,

---

17. Volo, "Powerful Poetry About Racial Discrimination."

sharing personal insights, and proposing solutions to address racial discrimination within a four-minute time frame.

A Blessing for Educators Committed to Racial Justice

God bless you
who see each person as an image-bearer of God,
who celebrate both your own racial identity and that of your students.

God bless you
who courageously sit with the discomfort of racial privilege
and commit to the ongoing journey of de-centering yourself.

God bless you
who raise your voice against racism
and learn the histories
and present realities of the racism your students experience.

God bless you
who, alongside your students,
stand in solidarity with those who find themselves marginalized.

God bless you
who teach in ways that honor each student's identity
and nurture a sense of belonging.

GUIDING QUESTIONS

- Break into small groups of three and ask one person in each group to guide the conversation.
- Take turns sharing one quote from the chapter that stood out to you. Explain why it resonated with you personally or professionally.

- Use the questions provided below as conversation prompts. There is no need to answer every question—let them serve as starting points to spark meaningful discussion.
- After the discussion time ends, come back together as a full group. Invite each small group to share one key insight or meaningful moment from their conversation.

Reflecting on Racial Identity

1. How do your own cultural or racial backgrounds shape your identity and experiences?
2. Were there traditions, foods, or practices in your household that celebrated your cultural heritage? How did they influence your sense of belonging?
3. What messages about race or privilege did you receive during your upbringing?
4. How have these messages influenced your understanding of racial justice today?
5. In what ways have you been conditioned to view whiteness as a societal standard? How do you think this has influenced your interactions with others?

Creating Inclusive Spaces

6. How might racial privilege shape classroom practices, such as curriculum choices, interactions with students, or discipline policies?
7. Reflecting on the anecdote about the teacher and the Asian student, what assumptions might you hold unconsciously, and how could you work to address them?

8. What practices or strategies can you adopt to make your classroom a safe and inclusive environment for all students?
9. How can educators foster spaces for students to share their racial and cultural identities?

Exploring Systemic Racism

10. Reflect on the idea that racism operates at individual, group, institutional, and cultural levels. How do you see these levels of racism functioning in your community or workplace?
11. What steps can be taken at the institutional level to dismantle systemic racism in schools?
12. Reflect on the concept of "death by a thousand cuts" regarding microaggressions. How can educators and students identify and address microaggressions in real time?

Becoming Anti-Racist

13. Based on the framework of becoming anti-racist (Fear Zone, Learning Zone, Growth Zone), where do you see yourself, and what steps can you take to progress further?
14. How can you encourage colleagues and students to join you in this journey?
15. Evaluate the representation in your classroom resources (books, toys, visuals). Are diverse racial and cultural identities adequately represented?
16. How can hearing stories about race and culture help students (and educators) uncover and address biases? Can you think of activities or assignments that would promote this practice?

3

School as a Place of Healing and Hope for Students Impacted by Trauma

Adopting a trauma-informed approach and practices can improve academic, behaviour, well-being, and life outcomes for trauma-impacted learners and their classmates.

—Jenny Williams and Amanda Broadway

STUDENTS IMPACTED BY TRAUMA

I still remember a cool fall morning when I was on yard duty, greeting students as they arrived. Since it wasn't yet time to enter the building, I directed students to their outdoor play areas to wait for the bell.

That morning, two young girls headed toward the front doors instead. When I gently redirected them, they quietly told me their father had passed away the night before, and they needed to speak with their teachers. I don't know how the rest of their day unfolded—our school didn't have a clear protocol for situations like this.

Pauline Naftel, a school principal of a Christian elementary school, has shared two powerful stories of how trauma shaped her personally and professionally.

The first is her own. When she was in third grade, her brother died in a car accident. Though surrounded by a loving Christian family and church, she struggled to understand the loss. She recalls wondering if it was even okay to cry—after all, "God gives and takes away." Her family rarely talked about it. At school, teachers and classmates didn't know what to say. Feeling pressure to carry on as if nothing had happened, she became more anxious. Looking back, she recognizes her behavior as a trauma response: fears, bargaining with God, and a desire to protect her grieving parents by being "the good kid." For years, she downplayed the impact of her brother's death, believing it wasn't a big deal.

Years later, as a school leader, she helped guide her community through profound grief. Most recently, a beloved staff member—a wife and mother to three students—died after a short battle with cancer. There was no protocol in place, yet the school responded with empathy, courage, and prayer.

Leaders visited the family, listened, prayed, and assured them the school would take its cues from them, recognizing that it was their grief journey first. Together, they planned the family's return to school. On the children's first day back, each class acknowledged their loss gently, offering love and support while giving the children space to talk—or not. Safe options were in place if the girls needed a break or someone to talk to.

Staff and the broader school community were invited to grieve together. Leaders shared the news personally where possible, offered space for collective lament and prayer, and sent a thoughtful letter to families with guidance on how to support grieving children.

Students were also given space to ask questions and reflect on how to support their classmates with love and sensitivity. Teachers prayed with and for them, coaching them to follow their grieving friends' lead, with permission to cry, laugh, share, or remain silent.

Tangible care became central: meals were delivered, logistics were handled, stories were shared, and support was sustained. Through presence and prayer, the school became a community of belonging, bearing witness to grief and walking together in love.[1]

WHAT IS TRAUMA?

Trauma is not defined by the events themselves but by the body's stress response to events that overwhelm the nervous system's ability to cope.[2] While trauma is often categorized as natural, man-made, or historical, it is ultimately the individual's response to these events that constitutes trauma. Natural disasters include events such as floods, hurricanes, and wildfires. Man-made disasters encompass experiences like war, neglect, and sexual abuse. Historical trauma refers to large-scale, systemic events such as genocide, homophobia, and racism.[3] Adverse childhood experiences are potentially traumatic and can have significant effects, including impacts on brain development, gene expression, and learning ability.[4]

STUDENTS WHO HAVE EXPERIENCED TRAUMA

We have always known that trauma existed; we may not have realized how prevalent it is in each of our classrooms: 61.8 percent of adolescents have reported experiencing at least one potentially traumatic event in their lifetime.[5] This was a statistic that was measured before the COVID-19 pandemic, during which more students

---

1. P. Naftel, personal communication, June 3, 2025.
2. Brummer, *Building a Trauma-Informed Restorative School*, 48.
3. Brummer, *Building a Trauma-Informed Restorative School*, 48.
4. Brummer, *Building a Trauma-Informed Restorative School*, 51.
5. K. A. McLaughlin et al., "Trauma Exposure and Posttraumatic stress Disorder in a National Sample of Adolescents," quoted in Burdick and Corr, "Helping Teachers Understand and Mitigate Trauma," 2.

were exposed to violence at home and experienced increased grief, leading to a rise in the number of students experiencing trauma.[6] With this in mind, the number of children who have experienced trauma has likely risen significantly since that study. Educators often underestimate the impact of trauma on their students, families, and colleagues.[7] Although as educators we are not qualified to diagnose trauma in children, we certainly can become more aware of the symptoms that our students may exhibit and apply trauma-informed practice.[8]

Children who have experienced trauma often experience fear, anxiety, irritability, helplessness, anger, shame, depression, and guilt. However, their ability to identify and express these feelings is often underdeveloped and poorly regulated.[9] Educators play a key role in creating a classroom environment that creates a safe space for children who have experienced some form of trauma.[10] As students continue to be affected by trauma, educators' awareness of the need for classroom intervention and support needs to increase. In this chapter, I explore how schools and classrooms can become places of healing and hope for students impacted by trauma.

SYMPTOMS OF TRAUMA

The first step in creating trauma-sensitive schools is to help educators recognize the symptoms of trauma. There are four types of stress response behaviors: fight, flight, freeze, and fawn.[11] Fight responses face the threat, flight responses get out of the way of the

---

6. Halladay Goldman et al., *Trauma-Informed School Strategies During COVID-19*, 1.

7. Evans and Vaandering, *Little Book of Restorative Justice in Education*, 31–32.

8. Burdick and Corr, "Helping Teachers Understand and Mitigate Trauma," 7.

9. Cole et al., *Helping Traumatized Children Learn*, 30.

10. Burdick and Corr, "Helping Teachers Understand and Mitigate Trauma," 7.

11. Brummer, *Building a Trauma-Informed Restorative School*, 50.

danger, freeze responses stay still, faint responses play dead, and fawn responses play friend to the threat.[12]

The most developed areas of a child's brain are the ones used most often.[13] Children who experience prolonged trauma suffer from toxic stress.[14] When children live in a persistent state of trauma, they may perceive school as threatening and constantly look for signs of danger.[15] In this state, their thinking brain becomes less accessible, and the brain stem takes over, responding as if there is an ongoing threat.[16] This keeps the nervous system in a constant state of dysregulation, leading to fight (e.g., aggression, arguing, silliness), flight (e.g., skipping class, daydreaming, ignoring), freeze (e.g., blank stares, refusal to answer, task avoidance), or fawn (e.g., perfectionism, lacks boundaries, overly helpful) responses.[17] Not all students with trauma-like symptoms may have histories of trauma. It is essential to consider all potential reasons for a student's behavior.

BECOMING A TRAUMA-INFORMED SCHOOL

"A trauma-sensitive school is one where all students feel safe, welcomed, and supported, and where addressing trauma's impact on learning on a school-wide level is central to its educational mission. This approach relies on an ongoing, inquiry-based process that fosters teamwork, coordination, creativity, and shared responsibility for all students."[18] Trauma-informed schools strive to:

- *Realize* the widespread impact of trauma and pathways to recovery,

12. Brummer, *Building a Trauma-Informed Restorative School*, 50.
13. Cole et al., *Helping Traumatized Children Learn*, 17.
14. Sporleder and Forbes, *Trauma-Informed School*, 20, as cited in Brummer, *Building a Trauma-Informed Restorative School*, 51.
15. Cole et al., *Helping Traumatized Children Learn*, 17.
16. Brummer, *Building a Trauma-Informed Restorative School*, 51.
17. Brummer, *Building a Trauma-Informed Restorative School*, 50.
18. Cole et al., *Helping Traumatized Children Learn*, 11.

- *Recognize* the signs and symptoms of trauma,
- *Respond* by integrating trauma-informed knowledge into all aspects of the system, and
- *Resist re-traumatization* by minimizing triggers and implementing supportive policies, procedures, and practices.[19]

In *Building a Trauma-Informed Restorative School*, Joe Brummer shares a story about a school where one adult failed to grasp the principles of trauma-informed care.[20] This adult would loudly and judgmentally call out students in the hall for being out of uniform. Brummer highlights three key issues with this approach:

1. *The Message*: In a trauma-informed environment, adults should ask *why* a student might be out of uniform rather than making assumptions. For instance, perhaps the student's parent was unable to do the laundry due to intoxication, or the child was taken into foster care following a parent's arrest. Educators are encouraged to ask, not accuse.

2. *Using a Loud, Judgmental Tone*: For some students, a loud, disappointed tone can trigger a trauma response, as they may associate it with past experiences of harm or punishment, activating fight, flight, or freeze reactions.

3. *Publicly Calling Out a Student*: Public shaming is harmful; few people, students and adults alike, respond well to being singled out in front of others.

Brummer's insights underscore the need for trauma-informed practices that foster understanding and empathy over judgment. It can be challenging for educators to step out of a situation and think of it from a student's perspective. In our own experience, we may have always had a working washer and dryer, and/or had a parent who washed our uniforms for us. That, however, is not the

---

19. National Child Traumatic Stress Network, *Creating, Supporting, and Sustaining*, 4.

20. Brummer, *Building a Trauma-Informed Restorative School*, 54.

case for all students.[21] A posture of curiosity rather than judgment would be more appropriate in a situation in which a student may be breaking a rule.

Amanda Broadway, in her role as an Indigenous Outreach Teacher, recalls a conversation with a student who stopped coming to school. The student shared that challenges at home made it difficult for him to get to school—his parents struggled with addiction, and he was responsible for getting himself there. After missing several days, a teacher warned him that failing to attend class would result in failing the course. The teacher's harsh, judgmental tone felt like an increasing burden, making it even harder for him to return.[22]

As educators, it is crucial to seek understanding rather than judgment when addressing student absences. The way a teacher responds can determine whether a student feels encouraged to return or pushed further away. Welcoming students back and having a plan in place for their re-entry can make all the difference in supporting their continued engagement in school.

Trauma can manifest in various ways, often leading to reactions that seem disproportionate to the triggering event. For example, a simple reminder about expectations might prompt a student to respond with inappropriate language. This heightened reaction could be due to the student perceiving the reminder as a threat, even if it was not intended that way. According to Brummer, this may stem from brain changes during adolescence or from past trauma.[23]

In *The Body Keeps the Score: Brain, Mind, and Body in the Healing of Trauma*, Bessel van der Kolk explains:

> It is much more productive to see aggression or depression, arrogance or passivity as learned behaviors. Somewhere along the line, the patient came to believe that he or she could survive only if he or she was tough, invisible, or absent, or that it was safer to give up. Like traumatic memories that keep intruding until they are laid to rest,

---

21. A. Broadway, personal communication, March 28, 2025.
22. A. Broadway, personal communication, March 28, 2025.
23. Brummer, *Building a Trauma-Informed Restorative School*, 56.

traumatic adaptations continue until the human organism feels safe and integrates all the parts of itself that are stuck in fighting or warding off the trauma.[24]

Creating a trauma-informed school requires treating each student and staff member with the assumption that they may be impacted by trauma, as we often cannot know who is living with its effects.[25] This approach means adhering to consistent protocols to ensure comprehensive care for everyone.

The ten core elements of a trauma-informed school include:

1. Trauma education and awareness
2. Identifying and assessing traumatic stress
3. Addressing and treating traumatic stress
4. Building partnerships with students and families
5. Creating a trauma-informed learning environment
6. Emphasizing cultural responsiveness
7. Emergency management and crisis response
8. Supporting staff self-care and addressing secondary traumatic stress
9. Developing trauma-informed school discipline policies and practices
10. Cross-system collaboration and community partnerships.[26]

Another foundational approach to addressing trauma, which encapsulates much of what we've discussed, comes from Souers and Hall in their book *Fostering Resilient Learners: Strategies for Creating a Trauma-Sensitive Classroom*. They introduce five fundamental truths about trauma:

1. Trauma is real.

---

24. Van der Kolk, *Body Keeps the Score*, 280.
25. Brummer, *Building a Trauma-Informed Restorative School*, 58.
26. National Child Traumatic Stress Network, *Creating, Supporting, and Sustaining*, 6–12.

2. Trauma is prevalent and far more common than we might assume.
3. Trauma is toxic to the brain, impacting development and learning in many ways.
4. Schools need to be prepared to support students who have experienced trauma, even if we don't know exactly who they are.
5. Children are resilient and, in positive learning environments, they can grow, learn, and thrive.[27]

STRATEGIES FOR CONNECTION

Building relationships with students is key to building trauma-informed schools and classrooms. Brummer suggests looking for needs, connecting before correcting, and considering the physical environment.[28]

Look for Needs

At times, needs simply cannot be met. Even in these cases, being seen and validated as someone with a need can be more impactful than having that need fulfilled. Empathizing with others, particularly children and youth affected by trauma, can reveal the underlying needs driving behavior.[29] For example, the student hiding under a table may be expressing a need for safety, the individual using strong language may be seeking acknowledgment of their anger, fear, or shame, and the student in a power struggle may need control. Needs are universal, neither good nor bad; they simply exist. Recognizing and interpreting body sensations is key in reconnecting the body with brain responses, which can be essential in trauma recovery, as trauma often disrupts this connection.[30]

27. Souers and Hall, *Fostering Resilient Learners*, 10–11.
28. Brummer, *Building a Trauma-Informed Restorative School*, 61–69.
29. Brummer, *Building a Trauma-Informed Restorative School*, 61.
30. Brummer, *Building a Trauma-Informed Restorative School*, 62.

Connect Before You Correct

Not taking classroom behavior personally is both an art and a critical practice when working with challenging behaviors.[31] This can be difficult, especially after investing hours in building rapport with a student who then responds to a friendly smile or hello by swearing, or when a student sleeps through a lesson you thought would be engaging and fun.

Building connections before offering correction is essential when working with students who have experienced trauma. Amanda Broadway recalls her time teaching in a self-contained behavior class for students who struggled to succeed in mainstream classrooms. Many of these students faced various challenges, including trauma backgrounds. She made a conscious effort not to take their behavioral choices personally, instead shifting her focus from rigid expectations to ensuring safety and addressing unsafe behaviors. Rather than prioritizing academic demands, she worked to establish a calm, trustworthy, and secure classroom environment—an effort that took several months to cultivate.[32]

Broadway recalls one student who had a particularly difficult home life, often arriving at school sleep deprived. Instead of insisting that he engage in academic work immediately, she allowed him to sleep for an hour or two, recognizing that he would be more prepared to learn afterward. Understanding students' needs—such as rest and nourishment—became a priority before academic engagement could even begin.[33] As noted in *Helping Traumatized Children Learn*, "In trauma-sensitive, safe, and supportive schools, students can experience their school as a safe haven, a place where they are greeted warmly by caring adults, can safely engage with peers, can explore their academic interests with curiosity and creativity, and be well supported to find success."[34]

31. Brummer, *Building a Trauma-Informed Restorative School*, 63.
32. A. Broadway, personal communication, March 28, 2025.
33. A. Broadway, personal communication, March 28, 2025.
34. Trauma Learning Policy Initiative, "How Can Trauma-Sensitive Schools Embrace Student Voice?"

Today's students face multiple challenges that contribute to instability and uncertainty in their lives. Many have experienced the disruptions of the COVID-19 pandemic, which affected their families and education. Others have endured natural disasters such as wildfires or floods, further impacting their sense of safety and community. Additionally, immigrant children and children of immigrants increasingly experience fear and uncertainty due to evolving policies that affect their families. Given these realities, creating trauma-sensitive learning environments remains crucial in helping students feel safe, supported, and ready to learn.

Everyone encounters stress, which can turn toxic without a trusted adult or supportive person acting as a buffer, helping to restore a sense of safety and control. This supportive figure must focus on the student being a human being rather than on their behaviors, which requires managing their own emotional responses first.[35] Just as on an airplane where you must put on your own oxygen mask before assisting others, it's essential to regulate your own stress before helping someone else manage theirs.[36]

Consider the Physical Environment

The physical environment can sometimes be a source of stress or even trigger a fight-or-flight response.[37] Brummer notes that "too much sensory information from the environment can be just as triggering as too little—students may be starving for sensory stimulus or their senses may not be able to take in too much sensory information."[38]

Consider reducing clutter, such as piles of books, papers, and supplies, as this may feel chaotic to some students. Additionally, bright fluorescent lights can be overstimulating, especially for those with trauma histories. Whenever possible, use natural light

---

35. Brummer, *Building a Trauma-Informed Restorative School*, 64.
36. Brummer, *Building a Trauma-Informed Restorative School*, 64.
37. Brummer, *Building a Trauma-Informed Restorative School*, 66.
38. Brummer, *Building a Trauma-Informed Restorative School*, 66.

with blinds for control. Sounds can also be triggering; loud noises like school bells may be distressing, while more subtle sounds, such as ticking clocks, air conditioners, fans, or even noises from outside, can add to sensory overload for some students.

LEARNING MORE ABOUT TRAUMA

The study of trauma and its impact on development is relatively new and evolving rapidly.[39] This chapter serves as just an introduction to trauma-informed schools and classrooms. Becoming a trauma-informed school requires evaluating every program, activity, lesson, and even movie choice through a trauma-informed lens. I encourage you to continue deepening your understanding of trauma and exploring effective ways to support students who have experienced or are currently experiencing it.

TOGETHER

Name

Material Needed: Photos of Various Images

Have photos available so that there is enough for everyone in the group to choose one that resonates with them. Each person chooses one photo that will help them tell the group about themselves. Once each person has chosen a photo, ask them to create a large circle. Ask one person to begin by sharing their name and photo and telling the group how the photo reflects who they are. For example, I once chose a photo of a swimming pool and shared with the group how I walk to the local swimming pool each morning for a swim.

---

39. Brummer, *Building a Trauma-Informed Restorative School*, 69.

Game

A "Window into Their World" Reflection Exercise can help educators gain insight into students who have experienced trauma.

Activity: "A Day in Their Shoes" (15–20 minutes)

Step 1: Scenario Reflection (5–7 minutes)

Educators receive short, anonymized narratives based on real experiences of students who have faced trauma (e.g., family instability, food insecurity, discrimination, or loss). Each scenario describes a student's morning before arriving at school, including stressors they may carry into the classroom.

Step 2: Personal Reflection (5 minutes)

Educators respond to prompts such as:

- How might this student feel when entering my classroom?
- What behaviors might this student display, and what are possible underlying reasons?
- How can I respond in a way that fosters safety, trust, and belonging?

Step 3: Group Discussion and Strategies (5–8 minutes)

In small groups, educators discuss their insights and brainstorm trauma-sensitive classroom strategies, such as:

- Creating predictable routines
- Offering quiet spaces
- Using strengths-based language
- Responding with curiosity rather than punishment

Cultivating Learning Communities of Belonging

Scenario 1: Maria (Food Insecurity and Anxiety)

Maria, a 10-year-old student, wakes up early, feeling hungry. Her family struggles to afford groceries, and she hasn't had a proper dinner for two nights. She gets ready for school, but her stomach growls as she boards the bus. When she arrives, she avoids eye contact and seems restless. During the morning lesson, she struggles to focus and snaps at a classmate who asks her a question.

Reflection Questions

- What might Maria need from her teacher at this moment?
- How could a trauma-sensitive approach help Maria feel safe and supported?
- What classroom structures could support students facing food insecurity?

Scenario 2: Jordan (Unstable Home and Hypervigilance)

Jordan, a 7-year-old, lives in a home where arguments and yelling are common. The night before, he heard his parents fighting and didn't sleep well. When he arrives at school, he is easily startled by loud noises, has difficulty sitting still, and seems hyper-aware of his surroundings. During group work, another student accidentally bumps into him, and Jordan reacts by pushing the student away forcefully.

Reflection Questions

- What is driving Jordan's behavior in this moment?
- How can an educator respond in a way that de-escalates the situation while fostering trust?

- What classroom routines might help students who experience unpredictability at home?

Scenario 3: Aisha (Grief and Withdrawal)

Aisha, a 13-year-old, recently lost a close family member. She used to be engaged in class but now sits quietly, staring at her desk. She doesn't complete her homework and avoids participating in discussions. When a teacher gently asks how she's doing, she shrugs and gives a one-word answer. Later in the day, she walks out of class without explanation.

Reflection Questions

- How might Aisha's behavior be a response to her grief?
- What strategies can an educator use to create a supportive environment without overwhelming her?
- How can a school community provide ongoing support for students coping with loss?

Frame

Video

Hosanna Wong is an international speaker, pastor, best-selling author, and spoken word artist helping everyday people know Jesus for real. Watch/listen together to Hosanna Wong's spoken word piece titled "Bernal Heights."[40]

---

40. Wong, "Bernal Heights."

Cultivating Learning Communities of Belonging

A Blessing for Teachers Working with Students Impacted by Trauma

God bless you who love your students,
without fully knowing the depths of their trauma.
God bless you who create spaces of safety
where students can begin to name their experiences of
fear,
anxiety,
irritability,
helplessness,
anger,
shame,
depression,
and guilt.
God bless you who seek understanding over judgment
when addressing student absences and truancies.
God bless you who realize, recognize, and respond to
the signs of trauma—
and who resist re-traumatization
by minimizing triggers and implementing supportive
policies,
procedures,
and practices.
God bless you who nurture learning communities
where every student knows they belong.

GUIDING QUESTIONS

- Break into small groups of three and ask one person in each group to guide the conversation.
- Take turns sharing one quote from the chapter that stood out to you. Explain why it resonated with you personally or professionally.

- Use the questions provided below as conversation prompts. There is no need to answer every question—let them serve as starting points to spark meaningful discussion.
- After the discussion time ends, come back together as a full group. Invite each small group to share one key insight or meaningful moment from their conversation.

Understanding Trauma

1. What stood out to you most about the statistics or definitions of trauma presented in this chapter?
2. How does the distinction between "trauma" and "trauma-like symptoms" shape the way we understand student behaviors?

Recognizing Symptoms

3. The chapter identifies five types of stress responses: fight, flight, freeze, faint, and fawn. Can you think of examples you've witnessed in the classroom? How did you respond?
4. How might understanding these stress responses influence your approach to managing classroom behavior?

Trauma-Informed Practices

5. What elements of a trauma-informed school, as described in this chapter, resonate most with your current teaching or school environment?
6. The chapter highlights the importance of not taking student behavior personally. How do you think educators can develop this skill?

Physical and Emotional Environment

7. How does your current classroom setup either help or hinder creating a trauma-sensitive environment? What changes could you make to improve it?
8. What strategies could you use to balance sensory input in your classroom to better support students with trauma histories?

Educator's Role

9. How can teachers effectively "connect before they correct" when addressing challenging behaviors?
10. What self-care strategies might help educators maintain their own emotional regulation to support students?

Equity and Inclusivity

11. How does addressing trauma align with fostering equity and inclusion in schools?
12. Historical trauma was mentioned in this chapter (e.g., racism, homophobia). How can schools acknowledge and address the impact of historical trauma within their communities?

Practical Implementation

13. What steps can your school take to begin implementing trauma-informed practices?
14. How can schools encourage collaboration between educators, families, and community partners to address trauma?

Student-Centered Reflection

15. The chapter discusses creating "safe and brave spaces" for students. What would a brave space look like in your classroom?
16. What opportunities currently exist in our school and classrooms for student voice?
17. What do our students say they need to do well in school? How can we learn more about what our students need?
18. How can you ensure that students feel seen and heard, especially those who may have invisible struggles?

4

Communities Where Sexual Minority Youth Are Seen and Heard

The struggle for justice requires attentive listening and looking—not ceaseless talking but, rather, listening with empathetic care to someone's description of being wronged.
—Nicholas P. Wolterstorff

HOW SHALL WE DISAGREE?

DAVE LOEWEN, IN HIS article "How Shall We Disagree?" argues that fostering a culture requiring individuals to choose between two opposing options is a form of reductionism.[1] He suggests that reductionism oversimplifies complex issues and reduces them so that one feels compelled to choose between two sides. If one chooses not to affiliate with one side of the issue, they may experience ostracization from both sides, and yet if one chooses a

---

1. Loewen, "How Shall We Disagree?"

side, they are not respected by those on the other side. In both cases, there are assumptions made as to who you are and what you think about a whole variety of topics. "In the end, reductionism takes away from the creative, thoughtful, and diverse representation that is the Kingdom of God. It reduces 'every tribe and every nation' to 'this tribe or that tribe.' It limits our ability to creatively and imaginatively seek the Kingdom 'on earth as it is in heaven.'"[2] There appears to be a growing shift away from humility toward increasing confidence and certainty in one's own opinions. In this process, we seem to have lost the capacity for curiosity about one another, prioritizing the need to assert and convince others of our perspectives instead.[3]

The gospel message is for us to love God and our neighbors. We have been invited by God to be a part of his story of restoration. As Christian educators, we have been called to model and lead students to participate in God's story. The way we disagree matters deeply. It is essential to recognize one another as bearers of God's image, deserving of our time and genuine curiosity. It also matters that we see ourselves as sinners redeemed by God's extravagant love, approaching others with a spirit of humility.

The current climate of Christian education in southwestern Ontario is one in which schools are becoming polarized over the issue of sexual minority youth. As a Christian educator, it is not my intention to take a theological stance on the topics of gender identity and students who identify as LGBTQ+, as that is beyond the scope of this chapter. I desire that as Christian educators, we can discuss how we might cultivate a learning community of belonging for sexual minority youth. In this chapter, I argue that Christian schools should create space for dialogue and learning with their school communities in how they can be places of Christ's love and hospitality.

---

2. Loewen, "How Shall We Disagree?," 3.
3. Loewen, "How Shall We Disagree?," 3–4.

UNITY—NOT UNIFORMITY

Perhaps one thing that we can agree on is that we are all image-bearers of a creative God. By starting with people and stories, we are reminded that sexual orientation and gender identity (SOGI) is not an intellectual problem but rather a lived experience for many Christians within our communities. In our classrooms, we are called to unity, not uniformity. As Christian educators, we need to educate ourselves on how to prepare to meet the needs of sexual minority youth in our schools and classrooms.

Abraham H. Maslow identifies "belongingness and love needs" as foundational to higher-level cognitive functions, such as learning.[4] Without meeting the need for belonging, students are less likely to engage fully in cognitive processes such as critical thinking and problem-solving. Multiple research projects show that students who do not have a sense of belonging are less likely to engage in deep learning.[5] Belonging is key to development and learning. We need to meet students where they are.

Some schools have created welcome statements that intentionally identify students as God's image-bearers and invite them into a learning space that values differences.

A welcome statement does not suggest that school communities will always agree with each other, but emphasizes the importance of loving each other amid differences. As educators, we have a legal obligation to care for all students, but as Christians, our responsibility goes beyond that, as we have been called to love our neighbor as ourselves.

---

4. Maslow, "Theory of Human Motivation," 381.

5. See Goodenow, "Classroom Belonging Among Early Adolescent Students"; Osterman, "Students' Need for Belonging in the School Community"; Spencer et al., "Stereotype Threat"; Walton and Cohen, "Brief Social-Belonging Intervention Improves Academic and Health Outcomes of Minority Students."

SOGI STATEMENTS

In his paper "Doing Justice Today: A Welcoming Embrace for LGBT Students in Christian Schools," Clarence Joldersma urges Christian schools to proactively examine their policies and community practices to identify and address ways they may be "marginalizing and harming students who are members of a vulnerable group," such as sexual minority youth, whether intentionally or inadvertently.[6] The language we use should switch from a reference to "them" to an acknowledgment of "us" representing the body of Christ.[7] Julia Smith in her paper "SOGI Statements and LGBT+ Student Care in Christian Schools" also considers the importance of putting together school policies about how the topic of human sexuality should be managed in one's school.[8] She recommends the following considerations in statements and policies with regard to SOGI:

> (i) ensure that all students—not just those who are cisgender—are credited with human dignity in the image of God; (ii) remove language that suggests students are choosing their orientation or gender identity; (iii) include language that calls out sexual abuse in general and harassment and abuse of LGBT+ students in particular; (iv) use more specific language like "same-sex sexual intimacy" in place of "homosexual behavior" and "bisexual conduct" or simply let the statement that sexual intimacy is only for male/female marriage suffice; and (v) avoid communicating an over-sexualized view of LGBT+ students.[9]

Applying these suggestions would allow one to focus on student care while leaving untouched the definition of traditional marriage.[10]

---

6. Joldersma, "Doing Justice Today," 41.
7. Joldersma, "Doing Justice Today," 44.
8. J. Smith, "SOGI Statements and LGBT+ Student Care," 290.
9. J. Smith, "SOGI Statements and LGBT+ Student Care," 301.
10. J. Smith, "SOGI Statements and LGBT+ Student Care," 301.

STUDENT CARE IN SCHOOLS

No matter what our thoughts are about sexual minority youth, our calling as Christian educators is to support and develop communities where all students can be seen and heard. Sexual minority youth in our schools face many unique challenges that put them at a greater risk of self harm and suicide.[11] "Rather than focusing on whether a person was born with these desires or not, we shift the attention to how a person can steward their sexuality as it is, and bring it to God for direction on how to have an integrated sexuality, by which we mean a sexuality that is integrated into the whole person."[12]

Emotion Coaching

The concept of emotion coaching comes from a desire for students to feel safe within the presence of educators—a space where there is a posture of openness to hard questions. Research on emotion coaching suggests that it is a credible, evidence-based approach well-suited for implementation in school settings.[13] Empathy is the capacity to see the world through another person's perspective, understanding the intentions, thoughts, and emotions that influence their behavior. This skill is vital for building relationships.[14] Our ability to understand and connect with others is shaped by our experiences, environments, and relationships. Emotion coaching fosters the development of empathy in children by encouraging adults to model empathic responses in their interactions.[15] We have students who have different beliefs and feelings about SOGI. We want students to know that they are accepted just the way they are and to meet their emotional needs so

---

11. Joldersma, "Doing Justice Today," 40.

12. Yarhouse and Sadusky, "Best Practices in Ministry to Youth Navigating Gender Identity and Faith," 9–10.

13. Gilbert et al., *Emotion Coaching*, 13.

14. Gilbert et al., *Emotion Coaching*, 27.

15. Gilbert et al., *Emotion Coaching*, 28.

that they feel safe in their presence. It is only then that the brain can return to its learning state.[16]

Emotion coaching involves five elements:

1. Be aware of a child's responses.
2. Recognize emotional times as opportunities for intimacy and teaching.
3. Listen empathically and validate the child's feelings.
4. Help the child to verbally label their emotions.
5. Set limits while helping the child to problem-solve.[17]

The model of emotion coaching does not come up with hard answers but keeps a posture of openness with students all around the three principles of having a duty of care, having a learning response, and being humble in our responses to students. Emotion coaching asks what the underlying emotion is. For example, a student may say that they feel afraid they are going to hell because they are gay. The student in this case mentioned that they were afraid. Anchor on them being afraid, giving them reasons for why them being afraid makes sense so that they feel heard. "I don't blame you for being afraid *because* there are teachings and beliefs about consequences of being gay might be. And maybe *because* what your family thinks of this they may have told you that is what happens. Those are very scary things to feel and I am here with you."[18] Let them feel validation and empathy. Meet their emotional needs at the moment. We want to give answers, but emotion coaching stresses that we need to navigate security before they are ready to hear answers.

We can draw inspiration from Jesus's posture of warmth and welcome. He did not condemn people but instead assured them of their safety and acceptance just as they were. His message was clear: "I know you, I love you, and I care about you." As educators, we have the opportunity to reflect this love by helping students

---

16. Gilbert et al., *Emotion Coaching*, 23.
17. Gilbert et al., *Emotion Coaching*, 46–47.
18. McVety, "PLC Sexuality and Christian Education."

explore and anchor their identity in who Jesus says they are, laying a strong foundation for their sense of self and belonging.

Pronouns and Washrooms

The use of pronouns and washrooms can be a couple of areas where schools will have a lasting impact on sexual minority youth and their view of their faith in Christ.

Pronouns

The use of pronouns is seen as an act of hospitality. Historically, these have tended to refer to a person's biological sex, but in today's culture, they can refer to someone's gender identity. One reason for this is that the meanings of words can change over time as well as vary from culture to culture. For example, in Canada and the United States, a game of football involves a ball in the shape of an elongated sphere, with tackling or at least touching involved. In most of the rest of the world, football involves a round ball with very different rules regarding acceptable contact. You do not have to agree with the use of pronouns that differ from one's biological sex, but it is a form of respect.

Some people argue that using pronouns that do not line up with one's biological sex is a lie. I disagree. We refer to people by the names of their preference all the time. For example, many people shorten their first name (e.g., Christine and Christopher are often shortened to Chris) or use a version of their name that may or may not include the same letters as the name documented on their birth certificate (e.g., Elizabeth is often shortened to one of the following: Liz, Lizzie, Eliza, Liza, Lisa, Beth, Bess, Lisabet, Lilibeth, Betty, Betsy, Libby, Ellie, Ella, Elsie). Using preferred pronouns is the same as using one's preferred name—even when it is different from that which is on their birth certificate.

Christian psychologist Mark Yarhouse suggests that allowing a person to choose how they wish to be addressed is an act of respect, even in disagreement.[19] Without granting them that basic courtesy, building any meaningful relationship with them becomes nearly impossible.[20] As Christian educators, building a relationship with each of our students is essential to cultivating a learning community of belonging. It is possible to show respect to someone and use language that reflects that respect, even when you disagree with them.

Washrooms

Schools should eliminate as many barriers as possible regarding washrooms. Renovating a washroom to be a family or single-use washroom is a positive and practical step toward hospitality.

Adopting a posture of listening, Christian schools are encouraged to approach each situation as unique, inviting individuals to share their needs and preferences. Together, they can collaborate to address any challenges related to the use of washroom facilities and find a resolution.

JOURNEYING TOGETHER WITH STUDENTS

Teachers play a significant role in considering classroom practices as they seek to understand each student's journey within the context of their human sexuality. We need to have conversations with each other about what it means to teach and learn in a community where our opinions about how to include sexual minority youth will differ greatly. I suggest that the starting point for these conversations be a posture of openness to learn more about the variety of ways that our students and possibly their parents are experiencing human sexuality. Ignoring these significant differences among ourselves shows a lack of understanding on our part. Just as we identify differences in students' readiness levels, interests, cultures, and race, so too, one's human sexuality needs to be considered as we set up classrooms that

19. Yarhouse, "Understanding the Transgender Phenomenon."
20. Yarhouse, "Understanding the Transgender Phenomenon."

are communities of belonging. Joldersma suggests "that a particular interpretation of justice from within the Christian tradition calls Christian schools to adopt a welcoming embrace of LGBT students. The assumption is that although other debates—legal, hermeneutic, and scientific—are important, the call of justice is more fundamental for the Christian community."[21] He writes that sexual minority youth should feel that they belong in their school without having to hide their sexual orientation or gender identity. One's sexual orientation and gender identity are an important part of a student's identity and as such an important aspect of who they are as a learner.

TOGETHER

Name

One Thing I Love

Share one thing you love that your colleagues might not know about. Some fun examples I've heard in include snow shoveling, painting, or making homemade cards.

Game

One Thing We Love

Form groups of three and take some time to share the things you each love. While many may agree that God and family top their lists, challenge yourselves to discover something more unique—something others might not expect or know about you. After your discussion, ask each group to share one love that all three members have in common.

---

21. Joldersma, "Doing Justice Today," 33.

Frame

A Blessing for Educators

God bless you who listen
With empathy and care
to the stories of others.

May your heart remain open
to the creative, thoughtful, and diverse expression
of God's Kingdom among us.

May the Lord guide you
As you live out the gospel—
to love God and to love one another,
welcomed into God's unfolding story of restoration.

And may you remember—
The way we disagree matters.

God bless you, redeemed by grace,
Who approaches others
With humility shaped by God's extravagant love.

GUIDING QUESTIONS

- Break into small groups of three and ask one person in each group to guide the conversation.
- Take turns sharing one quote from the chapter that stood out to you. Explain why it resonated with you personally or professionally.
- Use the questions provided below as conversation prompts. There is no need to answer every question—let them serve as starting points to spark meaningful discussion.

- After the discussion time ends, come back together as a full group. Invite each small group to share one key insight or meaningful moment from their conversation.

Belonging and Learning

1. Why do you think belonging is foundational for learning, as highlighted by Abraham Maslow and other research?
2. How can educators create an environment where all students feel they belong, particularly sexual minority youth?

Unity vs. Uniformity

3. What is the difference between unity and uniformity in a school community?
4. How can schools foster unity while honoring diverse experiences and perspectives on gender and sexuality?

Reductionism in Conversations

5. Dave Loewen critiques the tendency toward reductionism in polarizing issues. How can educators avoid this trap while discussing sensitive topics?
6. What steps can schools take to encourage curiosity and humility rather than certainty and division?

Policy and Practice

7. How can Christian schools assess and revise their policies to ensure they align with a vision of justice and inclusion for all students?

8. What might a welcome statement sound like while considering your own school's mission? How might it inspire changes?

SOGI Statements

9. Julia Smith offers specific recommendations for SOGI statements. Which of these do you find most practical and why?
10. How can schools ensure their policies respect theological convictions while also prioritizing student care?

Emotion Coaching

11. How does emotion coaching help students feel safe and supported? Can you think of a situation where this approach would be particularly valuable?
12. How might validating a student's emotions lead to deeper, more meaningful conversations, especially on sensitive issues like sexual orientation?

Pronouns and Washrooms

13. Discuss the importance of using preferred pronouns as an act of hospitality and respect. What challenges might educators face in this area, and how can they navigate them?
14. How does the way schools handle washroom accommodations reflect their commitment to hospitality and inclusion?

5

Indigenous Perspective Within Education

The decision not to decolonize—to continue with the status quo—is thus not simply a decision to prioritize other concerns or justice issues over this one, but a decision to actively (even if unknowingly and unintentionally) contribute to injustice.
—GERDA KITS

PLACE AND POSITIONING

I AM NOT INDIGENOUS to the land now known as Canada. I am a settler, who has benefited from a colonial system that has dominated this country for centuries. My parents are immigrants from the Netherlands, and I am the first generation in their line to be born on what Indigenous peoples call Turtle Island.

Today, I live in a place European settlers call Burlington, located in the Halton region. The lands surrounding the Great Lakes are rich in First Nations history. This area is part of the traditional territory of the Anishinaabeg, Haudenosaunee, Attiwonderonk, and the Mississaugas of the Credit First Nation, and it remains home to many Indigenous peoples. I confess that the Indigenous peoples I have named, and many more besides, remain largely strangers to me. By recognizing their long-standing relationship of care for this sacred land, I commit to joining the challenging, collective journey of learning, repentance, and action—a journey that seeks justice for Indigenous peoples and meaningful reconciliation.

As a Christian school educator, I understand that my position may be difficult for those with personal or generational ties to Canada's former Indian Residential Schools. I am grateful for the Truth and Reconciliation Commission (TRC) of Canada's calls to action, which highlight the need for education about the roles of churches and Christian school educators in colonization. The TRC also emphasizes "education for reconciliation," but it goes further, calling for the decolonization of education. I recognize that decolonizing education requires collaboration between Indigenous and non-Indigenous educators.

This chapter marks a part of my journey to educate myself about Indigenous peoples and explore ways to decolonize my teaching practices. As Barkaskas and Gladwin explain, "Educators must be prepared to feel uncomfortable and, as a direct consequence, integrate generative ways of addressing their own discomfort—without relying on Indigenous people as their primary supports—as they come to acknowledge their part in colonization. Mistakes will be made, and educators need to learn from them in the process of decolonization."[1] Recognizing this, I acknowledge that although I have done my best to support the work of decolonization, parts of this chapter may, unbeknownst to me, support colonization and/or be a form of appropriation. If that is the case, I apologize and am committed to learning from my mistakes as I engage in this process.

While it would be ideal to undertake this work in partnership with Indigenous people, it is crucial for me to first engage in independent research and develop a foundational understanding

1. Barkaskas and Gladwin, "Pedagogical Talking Circles," 26.

of Indigenous perspectives before entering into meaningful dialogue.[2] Moving forward, my journey toward decolonization will need to involve building partnerships with Indigenous communities, Elders, Knowledge Keepers, and/or colleagues to gain a deeper and more authentic understanding of Indigenous worldviews.

HISTORY OF INDIGENOUS RESIDENTIAL SCHOOLING IN CANADA

For more than two hundred years (1600–1800s), churches ran mission schools for Indigenous children that later became the residential school system run by the government of Canada and aided by the churches. Survivors of the residential school system have long known the injustices and horrors that occurred within that context. New recoveries of unmarked graves have once again exposed the magnitude of this devastation to the greater population and reached national attention with the discovery of 215 unmarked graves in the former site of Kamloops Indian Residential School in British Columbia, Canada, in May 2019.[3] Many Canadians were shocked to hear about this discovery, as the bodies belonged to Indigenous children as young as three years old. As of April 2025, the National Centre for Truth and Reconciliation's Memorial Register confirmed the names of 4,140 children who died while interned at residential schools.[4]

The primary purpose of residential schools was to eradicate the culture and language of Indigenous children, thus leaving a trail of intergenerational trauma among survivors and their descendants and generating misrepresentations of Indigenous peoples and cultures. This chapter will explore some of Canada's history of residential schooling to highlight the importance of decolonizing in Christian schools today. In Canada, decolonization

2. Barkaskas and Gladwin, "Pedagogical Talking Circles," 20–38; Chrona, *Wayi Wah!*, 23; TRC of Canada, *Honouring the Truth*, 239.

3. Carleton, *Lessons in Legitimacy*, 4.

4. National Centre for Truth and Reconciliation, "Residential Schools Memorial."

involves the active dismantling of colonial systems, structures, and narratives that have historically marginalized Indigenous peoples. This process seeks to address and rectify the deep and devastating impacts of both historical and ongoing colonialism, including the dispossession of lands and the overrepresentation of Indigenous people in prisons and child protection systems.[5]

Sharing this story of Canada's history is an important part of understanding why the story of Christian education needs to change. I will argue that listening and learning from our past as Christian educators must be a starting point to heal the damage inflicted by this system on Indigenous peoples. I will consider the practice of critical reflection in education to expose some of the unconscious assumptions, biases, and other forms of injustice perpetrated against Indigenous peoples in Canada to date. In doing so, I will conclude that Christian educators who are settlers need to learn more about the horrendous history of residential schooling to reflect on their current pedagogical practices critically and to expose forms of injustice that may continue to exist in Christian educational settings today. Decolonization, I believe, will help us teach more Christianly.

Before Europeans settled in what many people now refer to as Canada, Indigenous peoples were organized in hundreds of nations, with 619 such nations being named First Nations.[6] Following early European colonization, Canada's government also recognized the Métis, which means "mixed." The Métis National Council describes the Métis as a distinct Indigenous people and nation who were "originally the mixed offspring of Indian women and European fur traders. As this population established distinct communities separate from those of Indians and Europeans and married among themselves, a new Indigenous people emerged—the Métis people—with their own unique culture, traditions, language (Michif), and way of life, collective consciousness and nationhood."[7] Additionally, the Inuit constituted the smallest

---

5. BC Human Rights Commission, "Decolonization," para. 1.
6. Indigenous Services Canada, *Annual Report to Parliament 2020*, 11.
7. Métis National Council, "Frequently Asked Questions," para. 1.

group of Indigenous peoples in Canada, whose territory includes over 51 communities in the Arctic region.[8]

Federal laws and policies were designed to strip Indigenous peoples of their culture and rights.[9] This government recommended Indigenous children be separated from their parents to assimilate them into Western culture.[10] In 1834, the Mohawk Institute, run by the Anglican Church, became the first government-funded residential school in Canada.[11]

In 1883, Prime Minister John A. Macdonald authorized the creation of the residential school system.[12] Through this system, Indigenous children were sent to live in residential schools with the goal of stripping them of their culture, language, and identity.[13] Children attending residential schools were prohibited from speaking their native languages and were made to adopt the religious denomination with which their school was affiliated.[14] The racist assumption that Indigenous peoples were inferior contributed to the belief that they would highly benefit from being converted to not only Christianity but also European-style societies.[15]

By 1920, the government of Canada required all First Nations school-aged children to attend residential schools.[16] Throughout most of the twentieth century, residential schools were funded by the federal government and run by the Catholic, Anglican, United Methodist, and Presbyterian churches.[17] About 150,000 Indig-

8. Indigenous Services Canada, *Annual Report to Parliament 2020*, para. 33.

9. TRC of Canada, *What We Have Learned*, 5.

10. TRC of Canada, *What We Have Learned*, 5–6.

11. TRC of Canada, *What We Have Learned*, 22.

12. Joseph, *21 Things You May Not Know About the Indian Act*, 47; TRC of Canada, *What We Have Learned*, 6.

13. Chrona, *Wayi Wah!*, 23; Joseph, *21 Things You May Not Know About the Indian Act*, 41; TRC of Canada, *What We Have Learned*, 5–6.

14. Chrona, *Wayi Wah!*, 36; TRC of Canada, *What We Have Learned*, 7, 27, 51–53.

15. Chrona, *Wayi Wah!*, 37; Robinson, "Acculturation, Enculturation, and Social Imaginaries," 17; TRC of Canada, *What We Have Learned*, 7.

16. Joseph, *21 Things You May Not Know About the Indian Act*, 41.

17. Joseph, *21 Things You May Not Know About the Indian Act*, 49; TRC of

enous children are believed to have attended residential schools during this period.[18]

Many children were physically beaten and verbally and/or sexually abused. In addition, thousands of children died from disease, neglect, and suicide.[19] In 1922, Dr. Peter Bryce published *A Story of a National Crime: An Appeal for Justice to the Indians of Canada*, in which he exposed the government's neglect of Indigenous children's health, which included very high death rates of residential school students.[20] Even with this knowledge of the situation of residential schools, the government or the churches running the schools did nothing.[21]

By 1931, more than 80 institutions were running across Canada.[22] In 1969, the Canadian government took over responsibility for the remaining schools from the churches.[23] By 1980, thousands of Indigenous students were enrolled at the 22 residential schools still operating across Canada. The last federally run school remained open until 1996.[24]

On October 30, 1990, Phil Fontaine, the head of the Assembly of Manitoba Chiefs, spoke publicly of the abuse he suffered at Fort Alexander Indian Residential School, calling for a public inquiry that the federal government initiated in 1991.[25] *The Royal Commission on Aboriginal Peoples Final Report* was finally released on November 21, 1996, and recommended a public

---

Canada, *What We Have Learned*, 6.

18. TRC of Canada, *What We Have Learned*, 6.

19. Joseph, *21 Things You May Not Know About the Indian Act*, 46, 47, 50, 63, 68.

20. Joseph, *21 Things You May Not Know About the Indian Act*, 50; Miller, *Residential Schools and Reconciliation*, 17.

21. Joseph, *21 Things You May Not Know About the Indian Act*, 50.

22. TRC of Canada, *Honouring the Truth*, 64.

23. Joseph, *21 Things You May Not Know About the Indian Act*, 92; TRC of Canada, *What We Have Learned*, 6.

24. Joseph, *21 Things You May Not Know About the Indian Act*, 51.

25. TRC of Canada, *What We Have Learned*, 99; TRC, *Honouring the Truth*, 57.

inquiry into the effects of residential schools, including language loss and trauma.[26]

In 2007, the *Indian Residential Schools Settlement Agreement* came into effect. The government provided compensation to former students of 139 schools although certain classes of Indigenous students and types of schools are not included in the agreement.[27] On June 11, 2008, Prime Minister Stephen Harper, along with leaders from all government parties, apologized to former students, their families, and their communities for Canada's role in the operation of residential schools, and provincial and territorial apologies followed in the years ahead.[28]

The Truth and Reconciliation Commission of Canada was launched in 2010 to acknowledge residential school experiences, impacts, and consequences.[29] In addition, they were mandated to "guide and inspire a process of truth and healing, leading toward reconciliation" within Indigenous families, and between Indigenous peoples and non-Indigenous communities, churches, governments, and Canadians in general.[30] The process was meant to renew relationships that valued inclusion, mutual understanding, and respect.[31] The TRC hosted events across Canada in which thousands of stories were shared by those directly or indirectly affected by the legacy of the residential schools. The executive summary of the findings based on a multi-volume final report was released in June 2015. It included 94 "calls to action" (or recommendations) aimed at bringing healing to the legacy of residential schools and assisting in the reconciliation process. The TRC

26. Joseph, *21 Things You May Not Know About the Indian Act*, 94; TRC of Canada, *What We Have Learned*, 113.

27. Joseph, *21 Things You May Not Know About the Indian Act*, 94; TRC of Canada, *What We Have Learned*, 6.

28. Joseph, *21 Things You May Not Know About the Indian Act*, 51, 66–69; TRC of Canada, *What We Have Learned*, 99–100.

29. Joseph, *21 Things You May Not Know About the Indian Act*, 51; TRC of Canada, *Honouring the Truth*, 113; Miller, *Residential Schools and Reconciliation*, 147.

30. TRC of Canada, *Honouring the Truth*, 23.

31. TRC of Canada, *Honouring the Truth*, 23.

report characterized Canada's treatment of Indigenous peoples as "cultural genocide," as thousands of children died due to Canada's residential school system—with more than 80,000 survivors and their families still living with its legacy.³²

The tragic history of Canada's residential schools needs to be told with the help of the TRC's findings and calls to action. It is important for Canadians, mainly settlers, to hear the stories of survivors and learn what happened in these residential schools. Many of these schools were set up by Christian churches. As non-Indigenous educators, we should consider our responsibility in repairing the injustice of taking children from their families and acknowledge the impact of intergenerational trauma generated by the abuse and neglect thousands of children experienced under the banner of "Christian education." Jo Chrona suggests that "we need to feel as much as we think."³³ As non-Indigenous Christian educators, we should be challenged to ask ourselves what action we can take in our teaching practice to address the damage generated by the residential school system.

MAKING SPACE FOR INDIGENOUS PERSPECTIVES

Given the fact that our current educational system emerged from the Western understanding of education, it is safe to say that it is also the product of racist structures and colonial histories that define the West, preventing students from learning from a diversity of cultural perspectives. Committing to educating for human flourishing means working toward decolonizing the educational system. Education that disrupts the unfortunate consequences of our history should lead to action and actual change in behavior.³⁴ To make space for this kind of reconciliation, educators need to

---

32. TRC of Canada, *What We Have Learned*, 5; TRC of Canada, *Honouring the Truth*, 135–36, 370; Chrona, *Wayi Wah!*, 37.

33. Chrona, *Wayi Wah!*, 36.

34. Ng, "Complexities in Religious Education," 319.

engage in unlearning and relearning.³⁵ "Unlearning" involves putting aside false or incomplete histories that do not reference the Doctrine of Discovery, "a set of legal principles that governed European colonizing powers, particularly regarding the administration of Indigenous land,"³⁶ *terra nullius*, the assumption that land was not occupied, and are silent about the history of residential schools.³⁷ The role of the Doctrine of Discovery was rooted in a dysfunctional Christian imagination that shaped the worldview of European colonial settlers.³⁸ The historical narrative of Columbus discovering America is misguided as "you cannot discover lands already inhabited."³⁹

The history of residential schools is one that non-Indigenous educators need to acknowledge and lament. The work of the TRC shares Canada's history of residential schooling. The data collected and the stories told give us reason to lament the wrongs done by Christian educators. Only after non-Indigenous educators concede the truth of the harm that has been done can they consider the work of reconciliation. According to the report of the TRC, reconciliation must include the following four elements: (1) awareness of Canada's history; (2) acknowledgment that harm has been inflicted on Indigenous children and their families; (3) atonement for the causes; and (4) action to change behavior.⁴⁰ Christian non-Indigenous educators need to accept that all people are image-bearers of God and each of us is called to seek justice for all who have been marginalized and disenfranchised.

The 2015 report of the TRC describes current educational systems as ones in which racism toward Indigenous peoples is fostered. The report goes so far as to say that "much of the current state of troubled relations between Aboriginal and non-Aboriginal Canadians is attributable to educational institutions and what they

---

35. Farkas, "Canadian Decolonization," 6.
36. Charles and Rah, *Unsettling Truths*, 15.
37. Ng, "Complexities in Religious Education," 318.
38. Charles and Rah, *Unsettling Truths*, 15.
39. Charles and Rah, *Unsettling Truths*, 13.
40. TRC of Canada, *What We Have Learned*, 117.

have taught, or failed to teach, over many generations."[41] Hence, the TRC includes calls to action focused on "education for reconciliation." The first part of these calls targeting the educational system invites schools to teach students about the history of the relationship between Indigenous peoples and settler colonialism in Canada so that new generations understand how colonialism led to residential schools, and how residential schooling contributed to the challenges that Indigenous peoples face today. On a larger scale, this means one must reject the racism embedded in colonial systems of education and value Indigenous perspectives as integral to a new educational experience.

The second part of the TRC calls to action focused on education is more challenging as it calls for decolonization. The call is also for indigenization as it asks educators to consider how Indigenous perspectives and pedagogy can be integrated into the curriculum across all subject areas. Indigenization is the intentional integration and elevation of Indigenous worldviews, knowledge systems, and perspectives into various societal sectors, including education. This process moves beyond tokenistic gestures, aiming to meaningfully change practices and structures by incorporating Indigenous ways of knowing, thinking, feeling, and being. It involves recognizing Indigenous peoples as experts of their own experiences and actively working to dismantle power imbalances that perpetuate colonial dynamics.[42] Both decolonization and indigenization are collaborative and transformative processes that require the commitment of all people to create equitable and inclusive spaces that honor and respect Indigenous identities, knowledge, and rights. Before beginning these conversations in ways that are both respectful and constructive, educators need to have a good understanding of Indigenous people's values and ways of living.[43]

---

41. TRC of Canada, *What We Have Learned*, 234.

42. Queen's University, "Definitions," para. 5; Sloat, "What Does Indigenization Mean?," para. 6.

43. Kits, "Why Educating for Shalom Requires Decolonization," 200.

In responding to these calls to action, Christian educators may ask if they should decolonize. In many Christian schools, there are very few if any Indigenous students. With the many demands on their time, they may question whether it is worthwhile to decolonize their teaching practice.[44] An important factor to consider is that Christianity is not tied to one culture. The current educational system is dominated by Western perspectives, which represent one approach among many often rooted in colonialism and racism rather than a transformative interpretation of the gospel. Students benefit from learning from multiple perspectives in their classrooms.

Creating culturally responsive educational environments for Indigenous peoples is an important step toward addressing the harms of colonialism and the attempted assimilation of Indigenous peoples.[45] Decolonizing is one way in which we can honor and respect the original inhabitants of the land on which we live.[46] This is about a nation being responsive to the original inhabitants of this land. If non-Indigenous educators do not decolonize their schools, they will not only fail to restore relationships but also actively contribute to perpetuating broken relationships. Whether or not a teacher has Indigenous students in their class, they must work toward decolonization.[47]

Indigenous perspectives help prepare students to live a Christian life. By recognizing and acknowledging different perspectives or understandings than our own, students can better understand the complex relationship between the gospel and culture and how we might participate in God's work of restoration in the world.[48] For example, in Western culture, there has been a focus

---

44. Chrona, *Wayi Wah!*, 48; Kits, "Why Educating for Shalom Requires Decolonization," 187.

45. Chrona, *Wayi Wah!*, 27.

46. Chrona, *Wayi Wah!*, 42.

47. Chrona, *Wayi Wah!*, 29; Kits, "Why Educating for Shalom Requires Decolonization," 187–88.

48. Kits, "Why Educating for Shalom Requires Decolonization," 187, 239; Robinson, "Acculturation, Enculturation, and Social Imaginaries," 74.

on dominating the earth, leading to environmental destruction, while Indigenous peoples highly value the earth and how to respectfully interact with and care for it.[49] Indigenous peoples care about how people are interconnected and interdependent with the earth.[50] In economics, Western cultures focus on a depersonalized exchange between people where goods and services are often exchanged for money with no further obligations to one another. Indigenous peoples tend to follow the principle of sharing with those in need with no expectation of being paid back.[51] Today, many Christians have moved from the idea of dominating the world to being stewards of the world, being called to care for creation. As non-Indigenous Christian educators, we have much to learn from the Indigenous peoples who have been doing this for centuries. Decolonization may be considered one way to pursue wisdom in Christian education.

One of the most impactful ways for students to learn is through comparison. By engaging with diverse Indigenous perspectives, students can learn from fellow image-bearers and discern how different cultural elements align with the gospel of Christ. Christianity is present in many cultures, including Indigenous communities. Some suggest that diverse cultural perspectives can deepen our understanding of God.[52] However, it is essential to recognize that certain aspects of every culture may be incompatible with the gospel.[53] In Christian schools, students have the opportunity to strengthen their faith by challenging inadequate gospel interpretations. They can also cultivate a deeper relationship with Christ by appreciating how people from different cultures reflect God's image.

---

49. Kimmerer, *Braiding Sweetgrass*, 20, 25, 311; Kits, "Why Educating for Shalom Requires Decolonization," 196.

50. Kimmerer, *Braiding Sweetgrass*, 28, 166; Kits, "Why Educating for Shalom Requires Decolonization," 196.

51. Kimmerer, *Braiding Sweetgrass*, 132; Kits, "Why Educating for Shalom Requires Decolonization," 196.

52. Kits, "Why Educating for Shalom Requires Decolonization," 191.

53. Kits, "Why Educating for Shalom Requires Decolonization," 191.

Christian educators desire to live into God's story—a story of human flourishing in the world God created—loving God, our neighbors, and creation through our actions. We want to equip students to live justly and in peace. As settlers living on Indigenous lands, we must take responsibility for the broken relationships between Indigenous and non-Indigenous peoples.[54] Our pedagogy must encourage self-reflection and communicative interaction, leading to dialogue, questioning, and communication. John Dewey argues that we do not learn from our experiences but rather from reflecting on our experiences.[55] We must allow time for reflection as a means of transformation.[56] Teachers need to step beyond the assumptions that shape the pedagogy and structure of their educational practices,[57] confront their unconscious assumptions and biases, and learn how to engage respectfully with unfamiliar cultural norms.[58] Whether or not there are Indigenous students in one's classroom should not be the deciding factor as to whether students should learn about Indigenous perspectives. If we do not use history to learn from the mistakes made, we will likely repeat them.

INDIGENOUS WAYS AND RECONCILIATION

The vulnerability that leads to human flourishing requires us to take risks that may lead us to lose things we value, including a sense of self.[59] But when we look at our history, we can see that we have already experienced huge losses that we cannot retrieve. Decolonizing Christian education is a significant undertaking requiring collaboration between Indigenous and non-Indigenous educators. As non-Indigenous people, we need to overcome the racism and cultural stereotypes about Indigenous people that are deeply rooted in our

54. Kits, "Why Educating for Shalom Requires Decolonization," 187.
55. Dewey, *Experience and Education*, 25.
56. Giroux, *On Critical Pedagogy*, 46.
57. Giroux, *On Critical Pedagogy*, 19.
58. Kits, "Why Educating for Shalom Requires Decolonization," 193.
59. Crouch, *Strong and Weak*, 41.

lives. We should find delight in seeing each other as fellow image-bearers and appreciate the richness of different cultures. As individuals and institutions, we need to treat Indigenous people justly, as both treaty partners and original inhabitants of the land on which we live. This needs to be echoed in the context of the classroom.

Decolonizing Christian education requires that we create a space where all voices are heard. Pedagogical talking circles provide a structure that allows students to engage in reciprocal and relational learning.[60] Talking circles are used in multiple cultures, including that of some Indigenous peoples, as a pedagogical tool that encourages people to listen to other people's viewpoints that may differ from theirs.[61] This work is relational and is built upon knowing each other and celebrates both the individual and community.[62]

Indigenous ways of knowing emphasize student agency and collaborative learning, contrasting with the more teacher-centric approaches typical in Western education systems.[63] Indigenous practices foster learning that is communal, holistic, and interconnected, supporting both individual growth and community well-being.[64] The First Nations Education Steering Committee (2008) uses the following as principles of learning:

- Learning ultimately supports the well-being of the self, the family, the community, the land, the spirits, and the ancestors.
- Learning is holistic, reflexive, reflective, experiential, and relational (focused on connectedness, reciprocal relationships, and a sense of place).
- Learning involves recognizing the consequences of one's actions.
- Learning involves generational roles and responsibilities.
- Learning recognizes the role of Indigenous knowledge.

60. Barkaskas and Gladwin, "Pedagogical Talking Circles," 21.
61. Barkaskas and Gladwin, "Pedagogical Talking Circles," 21.
62. Barkaskas and Gladwin, "Pedagogical Talking Circles," 23.
63. Leddy and Miller, *Teaching Where You Are*, 33.
64. Leddy and Miller, *Teaching Where You Are*, 84.

- Learning is embedded in memory, history, and story.
- Learning involves patience and time.
- Learning requires the exploration of one's identity.
- Learning involves recognizing that some knowledge is sacred and only shared with permission and/or in certain situations.[65]

Two-Eyed Seeing/*Etuaptmumk*

Elder Albert Marshall, from the Eskasoni Mi'kmaq First Nation, is recognized for introducing the concept of *Etuaptmumk* or Two-Eyed Seeing to the Western academic context.[66] This idea was first shared within the framework of an Integrated Science Program at Cape Breton University in Nova Scotia, Canada. Two-Eyed Seeing emphasizes viewing the world through both the strengths of Indigenous knowledge systems and Western scientific approaches, advocating for a balanced and inclusive perspective that integrates both ways of understanding to address complex issues effectively.[67] It is the gift of multiple perspectives. For example, colonizers see Nova Scotia/Nouvelle-Écosse, Canada, while the Indigenous people see Mi'kma'ki, Traditional Territory, Turtle Island. It is not either/or, it is both at the same time. Two-Eyed Seeing emphasizes reciprocity, mutual respect, co-learning, and the integration of diverse perspectives to address complex challenges. These ways of teaching are more universal and more inclusive than traditional Western pedagogical approaches.

Two-Eared Listening

Two-Eared Listening is a concept suggested by Chief Joe, who suggests that before one can restore justice we need to listen to

---

65. First Nations Education Steering Committee, *First Peoples Principles of Learning*, para. 2.
66. Hatcher et al., "Two-Eyed Seeing," 145.
67. Hatcher et al., "Two-Eyed Seeing," 146.

the stories of injustice.[68] It "is based on the idea of learning and understanding, a willingness to suspend judgment and the desire to communicate respectfully in a way that might challenge previously held beliefs or assumptions."[69] Indigenous "elders tell us that we have two ears and one mouth so that we can listen more than we talk."[70] "By listening to your story, my story can change. By listening to your story, I can change."[71] Two-Eared Listening can be visualized by two ears joined together to form a heart. Active listening requires that we not only listen with our ears but also with our hEARts, which represents an open-mindedness that works toward equality and reconciliation.

THE IMPORTANCE OF DECOLONIZATION

Some people may fear decolonizing means abandoning what makes us Christian. They may be asking themselves: "How do Christian schools remain Christian *while* doing decolonizing work?" What I am proposing is a radical rethinking of this question. I argue that it is *in* being Christian that we decolonize. In doing so, we are striving to cultivate learning communities of justice and belonging. A school that functions as this type of community is one of close relationships that values each individual, is cooperative and collegial, shares leadership, sacrifices oneself for the other community members when needed, and accepts each other unconditionally. This community is one in which all the members work hard to agree on what is valued and understood. "It's a place where everyone is a crew member on a voyage and no one is a passenger."[72] In his book *On Christian Teaching: Practicing Faith in the Classroom*, David I. Smith writes that one of the most important Christian practices in the classroom is to create intentional

---

68. Joe et al., "Two-Eared Listening," 2.
69. Joe et al., "Two-Eared Listening," 2.
70. Moore et al., "Decolonization Through Two-Eared Listening," para. 8.
71. TRC of Canada, *Canada's Residential Schools*, 15.
72. Hekman, "Schools as Communities of Grace," para. 5.

learning communities that create space for students and their teacher to learn from one another and thereby model the body of Christ.[73] Believing that God created us in his own image and calls us to be the body of Christ, we need to embrace our differences and celebrate how God has made us each different. "When our lives have been transformed by God's grace, we see many things in new ways. And this seeing is guided by love, by an abiding desire to care about what God cares about—to rejoice in what makes God's heart glad and to grieve about what saddens him. That kind of seeing, *'beholding,'* has profound implications for how we view people and ideas and products and processes of culture."[74] This is the fundamental belief that should underscore our work in the classroom as Christian educators, the same belief that will make our classrooms inclusive, equitable, and just.

TOGETHER

Name

Before meeting together, ask participants to prepare to introduce themselves by reflecting on who they are, where they come from, and to whom and what they are connected—consider the land, animals, and one's relationship with Christ.[75] For example, I have responded to this prompt as follows:

- I am a daughter, sister, friend, wife, mother, and grandmother.
- My parents are European immigrant settlers who were born in the Netherlands. I am the first generation in their line to be born on the land Indigenous peoples call Turtle Island. I was born in the town of Newmarket, which is situated on the traditional territories of the Wendat, the Haudenosaunee, and the Anishinaabeg, whose presence there continues to

---

73. D. I. Smith, *On Christian Teaching*, 136.
74. Mouw, *Abraham Kuyper*, 92.
75. Prete and Lange, "Indigenous Voices and Decolonising Lifelong Education," 303.

this day. I recognize that I have moved around and that my European heritage has not nurtured in me a deep connection to the land or to the peoples and creatures that inhabited this land before European settlers arrived.

- I belong to my Creator. Through his grace and forgiveness, I have been given a place in his kingdom and am invited to take part in his ongoing story of restoration.
- My relationship with the land is one in which I find great joy from trees and natural outdoor spaces. I have a love for water and for the creatures in the wild (as long as I am a safe distance from them).

Game

One thing I have learned from Indigenous peoples is the importance of listening. All too often we hear people but do not really know what message they are trying to share. *Darts* is an improvisation game that requires listening and trying to understand what someone else is thinking. Darts is a fast-paced game where, in eight steps or fewer, the team tries to get two players to say the same word simultaneously by each choosing a word they think will connect the previous two words spoken.

Here's how it works:

1. *Setup:* The group forms a circle, and two volunteers step into the center. The entire group counts down from eight.
2. *Starting Words:* After the countdown, each volunteer says a random word aloud for the group to hear, clarifying if needed.
3. *Connecting Words:* Another countdown cycle begins, counting down from seven. After the final number, the volunteers each say a new word that they believe connects the two previous words.

4. *Repeat the Cycle:* If they don't say the same word, another countdown begins from six. This continues with the volunteers choosing words they think will bridge the gap between the words from the previous round.

5. *Tapping Out:* During the countdown cycles, any player in the circle can tap in to replace a volunteer if they believe they know the correct word. Even volunteers who have just been tapped out can tap back in if they think they've found the perfect connection, keeping the game dynamic.

6. *Restarting:* If the volunteers haven't matched words by the final countdown, they return to the circle, and two new players step in to start a fresh round.

In Darts, players rely on quick thinking and teamwork to find the perfect link and reach the goal of saying the same word.

Frame

Video

Watch Murray Sinclair on YouTube at "TRC Mini Documentary."[76]

A Prayer for Settler Christian Educators

God, forgive us
for the role we have played
in the harm done to Indigenous peoples and their children.

May we never forget
the horrors of residential schools,
a system that attempted to erase cultures and silence identities.
Let us name it clearly: cultural genocide.

Lord, open our eyes

---

76. Sinclair, "TRC Mini Documentary."

to see truthfully,
and stir in us the courage to take part in the work of truth and reconciliation.
Teach us through the mistakes of our past,
and bless our efforts in decolonizing education,
that we might teach in ways more faithful to your justice and love.

Bring healing
to this land,
to our relationships,
and to our schools.

In Jesus's name, we pray. **Amen.**

GUIDING QUESTIONS

- Break into small groups of three and ask one person in each group to guide the conversation.
- Take turns sharing one quote from the chapter that stood out to you. Explain why it resonated with you personally or professionally.
- Use the questions provided below as conversation prompts. There is no need to answer every question—let them serve as starting points to spark meaningful discussion.
- After the discussion time ends, come back together as a full group. Invite each small group to share one key insight or meaningful moment from their conversation.

Understanding the Problem

1. How do colonial histories and Western education systems perpetuate racism and exclusion in current classrooms?

2. What is the significance of the Doctrine of Discovery in shaping colonial perspectives on education, and how does it continue to influence us today?
3. Why is it important for educators to "unlearn" false histories, such as the narrative of Columbus discovering America or the omissions about residential schools?

Decolonization in Practice

4. What does decolonization mean in the context of Christian education, and why is it necessary even in schools with no Indigenous students?
5. The TRC outlines four elements for reconciliation: awareness, acknowledgment, atonement, and action. Which of these do you think is the most challenging for educators, and why?
6. How might integrating Indigenous perspectives and pedagogy change the way we approach curriculum and classroom culture?

Engaging with Indigenous Worldviews

7. How can the concept of "Two-Eyed Seeing" (*Etuaptmumk*) help bridge Indigenous and Western knowledge systems in education?
8. What does "Two-Eared Listening" teach us about how educators can approach reconciliation and dialogue in their classrooms?

Christianity and Decolonization

9. How do Indigenous perspectives on creation care, community, and reciprocity align with Christian teachings?
10. What would you say to someone who fears that decolonization might compromise the Christian identity of their school?

Practical Application

11. In what ways can talking circles or other Indigenous pedagogical tools foster more inclusive and relational learning environments?
12. How can Christian educators cultivate "intentional learning communities" that embody justice and belonging for all students?

Personal Reflection and Growth

13. Reflecting on your own teaching or learning experience, what biases or assumptions might you need to unlearn?
14. What does it mean for educators to see themselves as part of a "crew" rather than passengers in the journey of reconciliation?

6

Restorative Practices in Education

What has more recently emerged is the recognition that restorative practice also needs to be proactive, immersing the school community in a pedagogy that values relationships and a curriculum that values social and emotional learning.

—Brenda Morrison, Peta Blood, and Margaret Thorsborne

THE WAY WE DO THINGS

Early in my teaching career, I used to start the school year by creating classroom rules with my students. However, in truth, I had already decided what I wanted those rules to be and saw the exercise as a way to guide my students into "coming up" with the same rules that I had already decided on. In doing so, I did not listen to their ideas or value their contributions to our classroom community.

Over time, I have come to realize that truly listening to others is a gift: it allows us to encounter different perspectives that enrich our understanding and acknowledge that each person is an important part of our community. While listening may not always make things easier, it often makes them better.

This chapter discusses restorative practices as a means to consider how they can create a restorative culture as well as inform how one responds to wrongdoing or conflict.

RESTORATIVE PRACTICES

Restorative practice is a philosophy and approach rooted in caring, collaboration, and respect. It fosters and strengthens healthy relationships and community while offering a supportive framework to prevent, address, and repair harm through a continuum of practices.[1] The restorative approach is grounded in transparent, open, honest, considerate, and caring dialogue. It emphasizes the importance of truly listening to and understanding one another, resolving issues by considering events from others' perspectives and addressing everyone's needs.[2] By collaborating, learning about each other, respecting diverse perspectives, and valuing every voice, we can discover shared commonalities and use them as a foundation to strengthen relationships and build community.[3] Restorative practices can enhance the school climate, support positive discipline, and promote effective conflict management.[4] These practices aim to prevent suspensions, exclusions, conflicts, and misbehaviors, such as bullying.[5]

THE ROLE OF STUDENTS IN RESTORATIVE PRACTICES

A core principle of restorative practices is that adults collaborate *with* students to cultivate and strengthen healthy relationships and

---

1. Restorative Practice Consortium, *Restorative Practice Resource Project*, 10.
2. Restorative Practice Consortium, *Restorative Practice Resource Project*, 6.
3. Restorative Practice Consortium, *Restorative Practice Resource Project*, 6.
4. Lodi et al., "Use of Restorative Justice," 2.
5. Lodi et al., "Use of Restorative Justice," 1.

community while offering a supportive framework to prevent, address, and repair harm through a range of practices.[6]

Within a school community, restorative practices provide a framework for practicing restorative discipline and cultivating learning communities of belonging. The school community as a whole and the individuals within that community require high levels of structure and support. This creates a space in which students work with each other by cooperating, collaborating, taking responsibility, and being accountable to one another.[7] When classroom practices lack structure and support, they are considered *neglectful* and therefore lack student engagement. A high level of structure with a low level of support is experienced by students as punitive and authoritarian, thus representing a model in which things are done *to* students. Practices with little structure but high support are experienced as permissive and disempowering, thus representing a model in which things are done *for* students. A high level of structure and a high level of support, experienced as firm and fair or restorative, thus represents a model under which things are done *with* others.

In his book *Pedagogy of the Oppressed*, Paulo Freire highlights the importance of forging a pedagogy *with*, not *for*, the oppressed such that the pedagogical practice helps others regain their humanity.[8] He emphasizes the importance of dialogical processes for social justice and community development at the heart of the pedagogical ethos. Freire writes, "Authentic education is not carried on by 'A' for 'B' or by 'A' about 'B,' but rather by 'A' with 'B,' mediated by the world—a world which impresses and challenges both parties, giving rise to views or opinions about it."[9] Freire's pedagogical vision, as articulated in this quote, aligns with the model of restorative practices that aim to create a context in which individuals can take responsibility, learn from, and support each other through intentional interactions that include listening to one another.[10]

6. Restorative Practice Consortium, *Restorative Practice Resource Project*, 10.
7. Morrison et al., "Practicing Restorative Justice," 338.
8. Freire, *Pedagogy of the Oppressed*, 48.
9. Freire, *Pedagogy of the Oppressed*, 93.
10. Morrison et al., "Practicing Restorative Justice," 338.

Heidi Blokland, a teacher and principal in Williamsburg, Ontario, Canada, recalls trying a new approach with students who were off task or displaying inappropriate behavior. Instead of responding with correction, she began using the simple question: "I notice that you . . . [Describe the behavior without judgment]. Can you tell me what's up?" Then, she would pause and listen.

One day, while asking her fifth and sixth grade students to begin a writing assignment, she handed out loose-leaf paper. One student became upset, throwing their pencil and crumpling the paper. Blokland calmly said, "I noticed that you threw your pencil. Can you tell me what's up?" She expected the student to shut down, but instead they replied, "The paper is too thin, and I can't erase my mistakes."

Blokland describes the moment as mind-blowing. Instead of escalating the situation with demands, she discovered that the student cared deeply about the assignment and simply wanted to do it well. "It was so simple," she reflects, "and yet so powerful."[11]

Restorative practices suggest that low support and low structures lead to neglectful relationships. The word used to identify this relationship is "not." When individuals are given high support but little structure, the relationship becomes permissive and includes actions such as rescuing, excusing, and reasoning. The word "for" is used to summarize this relationship. When individuals are given low support but a high amount of structure, the relationship is considered to be punitive as it includes blaming and stigmatizing. The word "to" is used to describe this relationship. When one is provided with a high level of support and a high level of structure, the relationship created is considered restorative, with cooperating, collaborating, taking responsibility, and being accountable. The word "with" summarizes this relationship. Freire's use of "with" to describe restorative practices continues to be a worthy challenge for educators today.

---

11. H. Blokland, personal communication, June 9, 2025.

HUMAN FLOURISHING

Andy Crouch's work on human flourishing takes this idea of working *with* our students one step further.[12] Crouch writes about the importance of providing high levels of vulnerability and authority to bring us to a place of human flourishing. Actual vulnerability involves a story and risking something of great value that may be irreplaceable. Authority also consists of a story, "a history that shapes why we are choosing to risk and a future that makes the risk worthwhile but also holds the potential of loss coming to pass."[13] Both authority and flourishing are shared between people and are not meant to be private possessions.[14] According to Crouch's model of human flourishing, Christian educators need to engage students with high expectations, challenging them and providing them with a high level of support that includes vulnerability on the part of the educator. This will enable students to flourish in a way that contributes to the community's well-being, rather than merely replicating their own experiences.

What happens when we put these two models together is very compelling. As they both support and challenge students, educators must also be vulnerable to them. This use of authority in their role as educators is a way that leads to human flourishing. When we take a posture of openness and vulnerability, an image of intercultural encounters suggests a learning environment in which we move from learning *about* others to learning *from* them and finally to learning *with* them.[15] This form of hospitality allows educators to affirm their cultural identities and give others a welcoming space to be themselves.[16] I suggest that these combined models are a helpful structure as we consider the need to incorporate restorative practices into our schools and classrooms.

---

12. Crouch, *Strong and Weak*.
13. Crouch, *Strong and Weak*, 42.
14. Crouch, *Strong and Weak*, 47.
15. J. K. A. Smith, *Desiring the Kingdom*, 121.
16. D. I. Smith and Carvill, *Gift of the Stranger*, 92.

Today's classrooms are rich with students from diverse ethnic backgrounds.[17] As such, one of the best places to begin learning about the world is within the classroom itself. Teachers, students, parents, and community members all have valuable perspectives to share, and meaningful learning can emerge through the simple yet powerful acts of asking questions and listening to one another's stories. This practice serves as a crucial first step in addressing racism and developing a pedagogy that actively considers and uplifts those who have been historically marginalized and oppressed.

Integrating a restorative practice model alongside a framework for human flourishing fosters an environment where long-held assumptions can be challenged and decolonized. By prioritizing questioning and listening, students are given the opportunity to be truly known. Being known helps break down assumptions, nurtures empathy, and transforms how individuals engage with one another. This shift in perspective can have a profound impact on the classroom, reducing shame, stigma, and marginalization while fostering a more inclusive and compassionate learning environment.

I once heard a story of a class of students in Asia who were deeply invested in each other. When grades were shared with students those who did well shared a deep regret and disappointment in themselves because some of their classmates had not received passing grades. They felt that it was their responsibility as classmates to ensure that everyone in the class understood the concepts that had been taught. The failure of their classmates reflected their own failure to help their classmates. What if this kind of value and respect between students was found in all classrooms and not only in respect to academic success but also in terms of social and emotional well-being?

---

17. Cummins, "Teaching Through a Multilingual Lens," 12.

RESPONDING TO CONFLICT

The term "restorative" refers to how a person's or group's dignity, value, and interconnectedness are nurtured, protected, or restored in ways that allow them to contribute to their communities fully.[18] Restorative justice was initially developed as an innovative approach to addressing criminal behavior, aiming to reduce reoffending and enhance victim satisfaction. Since the late 1990s and early 2000s, when it was first applied in the field of criminal justice, its philosophy, values, principles, and skills have been adapted for various contexts, including schools and classrooms. Restorative practitioners working outside the justice system often use terms like "practice" or "approach" to avoid diluting the meaning of restorative justice as a distinct process. A restorative approach to offending behavior prioritizes repairing relationships and addressing the harm caused by assigning blame and imposing sanctions.[19] In this chapter, we will focus on restorative practices within schools and classrooms, using the terms "practice" or "approach" rather than "justice."

Zero-tolerance policies often rely on punitive and exclusionary measures, such as suspensions and expulsions, to address student behavior. Such policies typically focus on punishment rather than understanding or addressing the root causes of behavioral issues. While intended to maintain order and deter misconduct, these approaches frequently intensify disciplinary challenges, worsening outcomes for students.[20] This reactionary framework not only fails to resolve underlying problems but also risks alienating students from their school communities, hindering their academic and social development.[21] They can disproportionately affect marginalized groups, including those defined by race, gender, and socioeconomic status, amplifying existing inequities in education

---

18. Evans and Vaandering, *Little Book of Restorative Justice in Education*, 9.
19. Hopkins, "From Restorative Justice to Restorative Culture," 20.
20. Lodi et al., "Use of Restorative Justice," 2.
21. Lodi et al., "Use of Restorative Justice," 3.

systems.[22] These shortcomings highlight the urgent need for alternative disciplinary approaches that prioritize restorative practices and emphasize the well-being of the entire school community. By fostering empathy, collaboration, and mutual respect, these alternatives aim to create a supportive environment where conflicts can be addressed constructively, reducing the reliance on exclusionary tactics and promoting equitable opportunities for all students.[23]

Restorative practices have been a preferred way to resolve conflict in cultures such as that of the Indigenous peoples who put a high value on community. Over the past several decades, school communities have increasingly adopted restorative practices and approaches as an effective method for resolving conflict. More recently, restorative practices have been utilized both preventively and responsively to foster relationships, strengthen community, and support open, honest conversations.[24] The responsive approach emphasizes rebuilding and repairing relationships when necessary, while the preventative approach focuses on nurturing and establishing strong connections.

FOUNDATIONAL VALUES OF RESTORATIVE PRACTICES

Belinda Hopkins suggests that the foundational core principles of restorative practices emphasize openness, collaboration, equality, fairness, empathy, and personal accountability. These principles contribute to fostering a "restorative mindset" and underpin the approach's effectiveness in facilitating dialogue and resolution.[25]

While these five principles are not exclusive to restorative justice, their combination within this framework is what makes the approach unique. This blend of principles has inspired practitioners across diverse fields, providing tools to foster healing,

22. APA Zero Tolerance Task Force, "Are Zero Tolerance Policies Effective?" 854; Lodi et al., "Use of Restorative Justice," 2.
23. Lodi et al., "Use of Restorative Justice," 2.
24. Restorative Practice Consortium, *Restorative Practice Resource Project*, 6.
25. Hopkins, "From Restorative Justice to Restorative Culture," 24.

accountability, and collaboration in addressing conflict and harm. Hopkins suggests the key aspects of this mindset include acknowledging individual perspectives, expressing and listening to needs, focusing on impact, empowering affected parties, and building empathy and respect.

Acknowledging Individual Perspectives

Every person has a unique view of a situation, and it's essential to ensure everyone has the opportunity to be heard. A restorative classroom fosters an environment where individuals are encouraged to express their unique views, ideas, and experiences while also learning to listen actively and thoughtfully to others. Students come to understand that differing perspectives are not only natural but also valuable, enriching their learning experience.

This setting cultivates curiosity and a sense of wonder as students discover that even when they share similar experiences, each person interprets and internalizes those experiences differently.[26] Such diversity of thought and opinion provides opportunities to practice essential life skills, such as negotiation, compromise, and consensus-building. Moreover, students learn to appreciate differences, sometimes arriving at the understanding that agreeing to disagree is a valid and constructive outcome. Through these practices, young people develop social and emotional skills that are vital for collaboration, mutual respect, and community-building—foundational elements of a restorative approach to education.

Expressing and Listening to Needs

Creating spaces where individuals can openly share their thoughts, feelings, and needs while actively listening to others is a vital part of fostering connection and understanding. According to Hopkins, what individuals think at a given moment significantly influences

---

26. Hopkins, "From Restorative Justice to Restorative Culture," 24.

how they feel, and those feelings, in turn, shape their behavior.[27] Understanding this dynamic highlights the importance of spaces where thoughts and emotions can be expressed and acknowledged.

Using strategies like opening and closing circles in educational settings can help create such spaces. These circles encourage students to feel brave enough to share their vulnerabilities and connect with one another authentically. They offer a structured yet open forum where participants can make the invisible visible, bringing their internal thoughts and emotions to light in a safe and respectful environment.

Recognizing and validating the thoughts and feelings of others as important not only fosters a sense of belonging but also promotes empathy and mutual respect. These practices align with restorative approaches to education, emphasizing relational engagement and the value of every individual's perspective in building a supportive community.

Focusing on Impact

Restorative practices place a significant emphasis on understanding and addressing the effects of actions and decisions, rather than focusing solely on the actions themselves. This shift in perspective prioritizes empathy and consideration for others, recognizing these as essential for the health and well-being of individuals and the community.

Every action taken by students and teachers can have a ripple effect on those around them. Respecting others involves acknowledging and reflecting on the potential impact of one's behavior before acting. While individuals are not always directly responsible for others' emotional responses, since interpretations and feelings are shaped by personal perspectives and narratives—our actions and words undeniably influence the emotional and social dynamics of our communities. As interconnected social beings, our health and well-being are intrinsically linked to that of those

---

27. Hopkins, "From Restorative Justice to Restorative Culture," 24–26.

around us. When we consider the broader implications of our behavior, we foster an environment that promotes mutual respect, accountability, and a stronger sense of community. Restorative practices encourage this awareness, helping individuals recognize their shared responsibility in cultivating positive, supportive relationships and addressing harm in meaningful ways.

Empowering Affected Parties

Unmet needs are a fundamental driver of behavior.[28] When individuals experience unmet physical or emotional needs, they often struggle to function optimally, particularly in challenging situations. Addressing these needs is critical, whether someone has caused harm or has been harmed, as both parties often share similar underlying needs for resolution, understanding, and support.

Restorative practices emphasize the principle that those most affected by an issue are best positioned to identify meaningful solutions. Involving these individuals in decision-making is essential to finding a way forward that addresses the root causes of harm and fosters healing. Until unmet needs are acknowledged and addressed, harm may remain unresolved, and relationships may continue to suffer. By meeting unmet needs, we lay the groundwork for repair, reconciliation, and positive change.

Building Empathy and Respect

Fostering mutual understanding and respect through intentional reflection and dialogue is a foundational principle of restorative practices. Creating opportunities for empathic and collaborative problem-solving empowers students by affirming their voice and agency. Students thrive when they actively participate in decisions that impact them, as engagement with their own and others' thoughts, feelings, and needs enables more thoughtful, constructive choices.

28. Hopkins, "From Restorative Justice to Restorative Culture," 25.

In educational settings, when students feel a sense of ownership and alignment with a shared vision, they are more motivated and inspired in their work. This dynamic is transformative; it fosters a classroom atmosphere where everyone recognizes their role in contributing to the success of the collective. The shift occurs when both teachers and students commit to working together—planning, decision-making, problem-solving, and supporting one another when challenges arise.

This collaborative approach establishes a culture of shared responsibility, accountability, and high expectations. Within such an environment, the teacher is not just an authority figure but a co-learner, facilitating collective growth and success. For students, the classroom becomes a space of empowerment and mutual investment in excellence.

RESTORATIVE INTERACTION MODEL

A restorative interaction model in schools can be structured into a five-step process, focusing on dialogue and collaborative problem-solving to address conflicts or issues.[29] It emphasizes dialogue, empathy, and collective problem-solving, fostering a community-oriented approach to conflict resolution and relationship building.

1. Sharing Experiences: After initial introductions and setting expectations, participants are invited to share their perspectives of the incident. This allows everyone involved to express what happened from their viewpoint.

2. Exploring Thoughts and Emotions: Each participant reflects on their thought processes during the incident and describes how these thoughts influenced their emotional responses. This step encourages emotional honesty and helps others understand differing reactions.

3. Understanding Impact: Participants discuss the effects of the incident, identifying who was affected and in what ways.

---

29. Hopkins, "From Restorative Justice to Restorative Culture," 26.

This reflection fosters empathy and a deeper awareness of the consequences of actions.

4. Identifying Unmet Needs: The group examines the unmet or disregarded needs that contributed to the incident or arose from it. Participants articulate what they require to heal or move forward.

5. Collaborative Problem-Solving: Using the identified needs as a foundation, participants work together to develop mutually acceptable solutions or actions that address the harm and promote restoration. This collaborative approach ensures that all voices are valued in determining the path forward.

This process builds understanding, accountability, and trust, making it an effective framework for promoting a restorative culture in schools.

RESTORATIVE PROTOCOLS

By proactively investing time in caring for our students' emotional and mental well-being, we will find that the learning that needs to happen is done more efficiently and effectively than ever before. Using protocols is a great way to engage in restorative practices. These protocols give students and their teachers opportunities to engage in dialogue, show care for one another, and as a result create an opportunity for the class to flourish. Many teachers implement morning meetings where each student is acknowledged and welcomed at the beginning of the day in a morning circle. I have shared samples of these in the "Name" activity included under the "Together" section of each chapter.

Another effective protocol is the implementation of closing meetings where students could share with one another what went well and what was hard during the day. Although students are given the option to pass on sharing during the closing circle, it is a great time to reflect on one's social-emotional well-being and be aware of how others in the class are experiencing shared experiences.

A full-school quiet time after lunch break is another protocol to consider. During this time, students can read, draw, or sit, but they do not work. It is designated down time—a healthy habit that many adults would benefit from.

Although these seem like very simple procedures, it is sometimes a challenge to follow through on the commitment to do them. So often we try new things that are good for us and our students but then fall back into our old ways because they are easy for us and because we need to "cover the curriculum."

TOGETHER

Name

Have the group stand in a circle and respond to the question, "Imagine you are in conflict with a person who is important in your life. What values do you want to guide your conduct as you try to work out that conflict?"

Game

True for Who? (A routine for exploring truth claims from different perspectives.)

Step 1

Choose a topic in which there are differing viewpoints on your staff. You may consider one of the following:

Restorative Practices vs. Punitive Discipline: Which discipline approach is more effective in schools? Consider the viewpoints of educators, students, parents, and behavioral experts.

Grading Systems: Is traditional grading (A-F) effective? Consider viewpoints from educators, students, administrators, and researchers in education.

School Uniforms vs. Dress Code Freedom: Should schools enforce uniforms or allow freedom of expression in dress? Discuss viewpoints from students, parents, and administrators.

Cultural Representation in Curriculum: Should schools diversify their curriculum to include more cultural perspectives? Discuss viewpoints from educators, students, families, and cultural advocates.

Later Start Times for Schools: Should schools start later to accommodate teenage sleep cycles? Explore perspectives from students, parents, teachers, and health experts.

STEP 2

Reflect on the context in which the claim was made. Discuss the following questions: Who made it? What were the interests and goals of those involved? What was at stake in the situation?

STEP 3

Brainstorm together and create a list of different perspectives from which you could evaluate this claim.

STEP 4

Select one viewpoint to represent. Imagine how someone with this perspective would respond to the claim. Would they view it as true, false, or uncertain? Why? Take turns acting out this viewpoint, using the following prompts:

- "My viewpoint is ..."
- "I believe this claim is true/false/uncertain because ..."
- "What would convince me to change my opinion is ..."

Step 5

Step outside the circle of viewpoints and consider everything you've heard. What is your final conclusion or stance? What new ideas or questions have emerged?

Frame

Videos

Watch a video about restorative practices together. Consider one of the following:

- Restorative Practices: Circles in the Classroom (2:04)[30]
- Restorative Practices: Students' Perspectives (1:59)[31]

A Blessing for Educators Committed to Restorative Ways

God bless you
whose work is grounded in care,
collaboration, and mutual respect.
May your efforts nurture strong, healthy relationships
and build communities where harm is prevented, addressed, and healed with grace.

God bless you
who take time to learn from one another,
who honor diverse perspectives
and uplift every voice.
As you uncover shared truths,
may they become the foundation
for deeper connection and lasting community.

---

30. Fisher and Frey, "Restorative Practices: Circles in the Classroom."
31. Fisher and Frey, "Restorative Practices: Students' Perspectives."

God bless you
who work *with* your students,
fostering spaces of belonging,
where relationships grow strong
and grace flows freely.

GUIDING QUESTIONS

- Break into small groups of three and ask one person in each group to guide the conversation.
- Take turns sharing one quote from the chapter that stood out to you. Explain why it resonated with you personally or professionally.
- Use the questions provided below as conversation prompts. There is no need to answer every question—let them serve as starting points to spark meaningful discussion.
- After the discussion time ends, come back together as a full group. Invite each small group to share one key insight or meaningful moment from their conversation.

Understanding Restorative Practices

1. How do you define "restorative practices" in your own words, based on what you read in the chapter?
2. How do the principles of restorative practices align with Paulo Freire's idea of working "with" students rather than "for" or "to" them?
3. In what ways do morning or closing meetings, as described in the chapter, contribute to a restorative classroom culture?

Reflection on Experiences

4. Reflect on your own educational experience as a student or educator. Were there moments when you saw restorative practices in action? If not, what might have changed in those situations if a restorative approach had been applied?
5. The chapter highlights the importance of creating high structure and high support environments. Can you think of examples of classrooms or schools that excelled at this? What stood out about those spaces?

Building Relationships and Community

6. The chapter emphasizes the value of listening and learning *with* others. How can teachers model this approach in their classrooms?

Application to Teaching Practice

7. What steps can educators take to ensure that restorative practices become a proactive part of their classroom routines, rather than just a response to conflict?
8. How can educators balance the time spent on restorative practices with the pressure to "cover the curriculum"?

Connection to Broader Themes

9. Andy Crouch's model of human flourishing highlights the importance of both vulnerability and authority. How can educators embody these traits to foster flourishing in their classrooms?

Responses to Conflict

10. What are the main differences between a restorative approach and a punitive or zero-tolerance policy?
11. How does a restorative model address the root causes of conflict differently than traditional disciplinary models?

Practical Scenarios

12. Imagine a student has caused harm to a classmate. Using the five-step restorative interaction model, how might you facilitate a restorative dialogue between them?
13. Think about your classroom or school context. What unmet needs among students might contribute to conflicts, and how could restorative practices help address them?

Inclusivity and Equity

14. Restorative practices are rooted in the value of diversity and community. How can they help decolonize assumptions and promote equity in schools?
15. The chapter references the story of students in Asia who felt responsible for each other's success. How can we cultivate this sense of shared responsibility in classrooms that value individualism?

7

Pedagogy and Community

I needed material that would not just illustrate a verb form or a dialogue context, but that showed speakers of the target language as believers, choosers, and sufferers, as those who yearn, celebrate, and mourn. I needed images and stories of people that invited us to learn *from* them and not just *about* them.
—David I. Smith

UBUNTU: I AM BECAUSE WE ARE[1]

THERE IS A STORY about a western anthropologist who interacted with a group of children in South Africa. He placed a basket of sweet fruit near a tree and had the children stand several meters away. He told the children that whoever got to the basket of fruit first would get to keep it all to themselves. He then started the race, "On your mark, get set, go!" What these children did surprised him. They held each other's hands and then ran toward the tree and basket of fruit together. In this way, they were all able to share

---

1. van der Boom, "Ubuntu."

the fruit. The anthropologist asked them why they ran the race that way. Their response was "*Ubuntu*. How can one be happy when all the others are sad?" *Ubuntu*, which comes from the Zulu and Xhosa languages, represents a South African ethical ideology that focuses on people's relationships and partnerships with each other. It means "I am because we are."

I believe that the philosophy of *Ubuntu* can help us dig into an essential element of the vision of Christian Deeper Learning: celebrating learners as God's image-bearers, particularly in the context of a classroom community.

It is important for students to know what it means to be created in the image of God and to impress on them the high calling this gives them. The paradox in education arises as we strive to emphasize not just the value of each individual but also that of the community of learners. Good education allows opportunities for both to be nurtured and celebrated.

CHRISTIAN DEEPER LEARNING

Deeper learning can be defined as the practice of applying what is learned to new situations. The skills involved in such learning include critical thinking and problem solving, communication, collaboration, and learning to learn. Students engaged in deeper learning are not simply developing cognitive skills; they are also cultivating interpersonal and intrapersonal competencies. Celebrating each other, as opposed to simply pursuing and celebrating individual achievements, confirms for students their value and the importance of their contributions.

Christian Deeper Learning emphasizes celebrating each learner, intentionally designing learning experiences, and cultivating a culture where teaching practices equip students to live out God's story through meaningful work that shapes both their identity and the world around them.[2] Ultimately, our goal is to

---

2. Christian Deeper Learning, "About Us."

help students learn to love God and their neighbors in their daily lives—not just in the future, but right now.

Justin Cook and Darryl DeBoer proposed the following definition for deeper learning within the context of Christian education: "People of God's story engaged in real work that forms self and shapes the world."[3] As Christians we are called to love God and love others. Another way of putting this may be to say that we are image-bearers of God, who are interconnected, called to love our neighbors and care for our broken world as part of God's story of redemption. Shifting education from knowledge transfer to learner formation is in alignment with this idea, as it puts the learner first, giving more value to the person than to the subject matter.

David I. Smith writes, "Christian faith can motivate the intentional design of patterns of practice within particular contexts, with the goal of telling the same story through our practices that we profess with our lips."[4] Our Christian faith should be reflected in the ways we teach and interact with students. Smith invites us to reimagine our classrooms in light of core Christian values—seeing them as spaces shaped by grace, justice, beauty, joy, virtue, and the enduring presence of faith, hope, and love.[5] As Christian educators though our faith is foundational to all we do, and our desire to obey God and follow in his ways means so much more than being a good educator. It is a privilege to work in a Christian school where we can be explicit about our beliefs and talk about how to live that out with our students. Christian Deeper Learning offers a framework that nurtures our students' growth in Christlike character, encouraging them to serve others and care for the world around them. As Christians, we should lead the way in deeper learning. So much of what we teach in the classroom comes from a research-based curriculum, and for that we are thankful. Applying deeper learning comes from a desire to be intentional about making what is learned meaningful. There is so much brokenness in the world, and God has called us to be part of his redemptive

---

3. Cook and DeBoer, "Deeper Learning in Christian Education," 13.
4. D. I. Smith, *On Christian Teaching*, 68.
5. D. I. Smith, *On Christian Teaching*, 71.

work. Christian Deeper Learning gives us a structure to fulfill the work he is calling us to do.

INTERCONNECTED AS IMAGE-BEARERS

Christian Deeper Learning encourages learners to be more inclusive of others, both in their classroom and around the world. Too often, as educators, we think that our job requires us to have all the answers and solutions to problems. With that mindset, we miss out on the opportunity to learn together with our students. Optimism, hope, and generosity can be challenging to hold on to when we work alone, but within the context of a community, they can grow beyond ourselves. Cultivating learning communities of belonging means that we truly value each person's voice and opinion. Considering learning to be a communal activity rather than just an individual activity really resonates with me. Learning this way goes way beyond our own individual goals and desires and looks at what would be beneficial to others and to the world in which we live as we consider the impact of our learning and actions from a just perspective. Collaboration celebrates and values our identity as a member of Christ's body. Learning should not be teacher-focused, but neither should it be entirely student-focused. When teachers and students collaborate, learning is rich and meaningful for all. They each play a part in the learning journey.

Intentionally having students develop their interpersonal and intrapersonal competencies for better learning is an area that has not always been given the attention it deserves. Group work has often been assigned with a focus merely on meeting academic goals rather than on truly building the social-emotional skills that students need. Fortunately, over the last few years, and especially as a result of the COVID-19 pandemic, students' mental health and interpersonal skills are getting more attention. I think that how we authentically value each student has a greater impact on learning than we have given it credit for. Valuing students as God's image-bearers and as members of a collaborative learning community requires more than acknowledgment—it needs to be integrated into the ways that we design and celebrate learning.

When I think of loving my neighbor, I think that subconsciously I have been identifying my neighbor as those people who look and act like me. My neighbors do not act or look so different from me. A couple of years ago, my husband and I spent time in Zambia as International Relief Managers on behalf of World Renew. We spent months in a very small village where we were sometimes the only white people around. At times the children would call out on the street, "white person, white person" in their own language. Within that context I often wished that my skin color was darker so that I could fit in with everyone else.

In *Pedagogy of the Oppressed*, Freire considers the position of the marginalized and suggests that their differences can be considered a deterrent in achieving success.[6] We so want to be like those around us rather than celebrating the fact that we have each been created differently for the good of the whole. It will take much open and honest conversation to help us move from being so unaware of our racial and cultural differences to a place where we can celebrate them. Although we may not know exactly how this will play out, we must get these conversations going.

It is important to recognize that the culture of a school grows out of people's beliefs and values.[7] The core belief of Christian school teachers is that all human beings are worthy and interconnected as image-bearers of God. As a result, we strive to create just and equitable learning environments that nurture healthy relationships that repair harm and transform conflict.[8] "Justice is embodied in how we live together as a community, how we support, encourage, and nurture each other. It is holistic, impacting all aspects of our society."[9] When reflecting on whether our actions

---

6. Freire, *Pedagogy of the Oppressed*, 157.

7. Evans and Vaandering, *Little Book of Restorative Justice in Education*, 33–34.

8. Evans and Vaandering, *Little Book of Restorative Justice in Education*, 58, 67.

9. Evans and Vaandering, *Little Book of Restorative Justice in Education*, 17.

align with these values, Katherine Evans and Dorothy Vaandering suggest we consider the following questions:

- In my interactions with others and the world, do I offer respect by accepting them as they are, or do I try to change them to fit my needs or expectations?
- Do I treat others with dignity, engaging with them in a way that brings out their best qualities?
- Am I aware of what others need to survive and thrive?
- Do I ensure that I am not hindering someone else's well-being?
- Do I actively engage with others to support their well-being and help them flourish?
- Can I recognize how my responses to these questions reflect my relationship with myself?[10]

Christian Deeper Learning is a learning framework that supports Christian educators' desire to encourage our students to live out their calling as image-bearers to serve neighbors and care for creation. Cook and DeBoer write, "The pursuit of deeper learning in Christian schools must find its anchor in the role of story as a key design principle. Our curriculum finds its meaning and purpose within God's unfolding story: a story of redemption that invites us to participate, to co-create with God, in the restoration of a broken but beautiful and delightful world."[11] Christian Deeper Learning emphasizes real work for real people who have a real need to connect their stories to God's story of restoration for the world.

With so much brokenness in the world, God calls us to be part of his restorative work. Together with my students, I am being challenged to look inward at my own heart and mind to see what I am currently doing that is hurtful and unjust. Once I become more aware of my own injustices, I will be better prepared to look outward to see what needs to be done in the world, thinking of my call to do what is just and to show mercy. When we apply what

---

10. Evans and Vaandering, *Little Book of Restorative Justice in Education*, 39.
11. Cook and DeBoer, "Deeper Learning in Christian Education," 14.

we know to the real world, we find ourselves being shaped by the actions that we take.

The United Nations has challenged educators to teach students how to be global citizens. They state, "By 2030, ensure that all learners acquire the knowledge and skills needed to promote ... human rights, gender equity, promotion of a culture of peace and non-violence, global citizenship and appreciation of cultural diversity and of culture's contribution to sustainable development."[12] The goal is not limited to college and university students or even secondary students. It is a call for all learners. As Christians we are called to be transformers of society and culture by seeking justice and righteousness for those who are marginalized and disenfranchised. Our identity in Christ gives us the framework from which we can build signature pedagogies that include our interconnectedness as the body of Christ, our call to love God and love our neighbors, and being a part of God's story in doing justice, loving kindness, and walking humbly with him.

EXAMPLES OF CHRISTIAN DEEPER LEARNING

In the following paragraphs, I offer some examples of models of Christian Deeper Learning. I share these specifically as they are ones that have been shared with me that to some degree meet the expectations of real work that meets a real need for real people.

On a visit to Malawi, Africa (April 2024), an educator told me a story about how students in the northern part were concerned about the children in the southern part of the country. He explained that those in south Malawi had experienced significant flooding and as a result lost both their homes and personal belongings. The students in the north, while also experiencing poverty, organized a clothes drive to collect clothes from their families and neighbors to donate to those who needed them in the south. They organized this activity for those who had been devastated by the flood.

---

12. UNESCO, *Education for People and Planet*, 287.

Other school leaders in Malawi believed that working as Christian educators goes beyond teaching and learning. As a result, they encouraged the school to grow vegetation around their school to show the beauty of God's creation to their learning community. In their classrooms, school leaders have started to think more about creating equitable space for all. The equal treatment of learners showed that all were valued as God's image-bearers.

Early in her teaching career, Angie Bonvanie, a teacher at Halton Hills Christian School in Georgetown, Ontario, Canada, grew frustrated when her students frequently asked, *"Is this good enough?"* before submitting assignments. Everything changed when she provided her students with an authentic audience and purpose for their work. Her grade five and six students, who had previously struggled with completing assignments and engaging in the writing process, became highly motivated when tasked with writing stories about enslaved individuals. These stories were later published as a book. The class chose to donate the book's proceeds to the International Justice Mission, an organization dedicated to rescuing victims of slavery.[13]

At the Arsi Negele School in Ethiopia, elementary students learning about stewardship in their science class formed an Earth Keepers Club.[14] As a club, they planted trees in the school compound and took on the responsibility of watering them regularly. They were motivated to care for the earth right where they were.

Students from Amrahiah Community School in Ghana, while learning about the environment and sanitation, organized a community clean-up. They picked up litter in their local community for a few hours a couple of times a year.[15]

Grade eleven biology students from Surrey, British Columbia, Canada, cared for a local urban forest (Tynehead Regional Park and salmon hatchery) as they studied flora and fauna. Their

---

13. A. Bonvanie, personal communication, December 5, 2024.
14. Amosu, "Green Disciples."
15. E. Vandergrift, personal communication, March 1, 2024.

work led them to lead tours that allowed others to appreciate the park's flora and fauna and encouraged them to care for it.[16]

Carla Alblas, a grade seven teacher in Dundas, Ontario, Canada, challenged her students to consider what it means to be a good neighbor, both locally and globally. Her curriculum incorporated three powerful questions, guiding students to connect with their community's past, present, and the wider world.[17]

To help students understand "Who are my historical neighbors and how can we show them love?" Alblas initiated a collaboration with the local museum. As part of their studies on structures, students delved into the history of Dundas's old buildings. They uncovered fascinating stories about these landmarks, learning about their original purposes and how they're utilized today. Through these narratives, students gained insight into the lives of early Dundas residents and the town's historical development. They then chose a historical figure and drew connections to the broader narrative of Confederation.

Alblas also prompted her students to respond to the question "Who are my marginalized neighbors and how can we show them love?" This led them to engage with elderly residents in local retirement homes. By gathering and recording the seniors' life stories, the students compiled and published a book. This project instilled a strong sense of purpose in their writing, as the knowledge that their work would be shared with an authentic audience motivated them to prioritize accuracy in spelling, grammar, and overall quality.

For the question "Who are my global neighbors and how can we show them love?" the grade seven students partnered with EduDeo, an organization committed to advancing Christ-centered education globally. Through this partnership, students researched global water issues and successfully raised funds to support a clean water project, demonstrating their commitment to making a difference beyond their immediate community.

---

16. E. Vandergrift, personal communication, March 1, 2024.
17. C. Alblas, personal communication, March 5, 2024.

All of the examples of Christian Deeper Learning above involve teachers and students each playing a part in the learning community. When they co-create, the learning is rich and meaningful for all.

HIERARCHY OF AUDIENCE

Traditionally schooling has long required students to complete assigned work for the teacher who gave it. Ron Berger et al. suggest the following hierarchy of audience:

- "To present to a teacher to fulfill a requirement.
- To present to parents.
- To present to the school community.
- To present to a public audience beyond the school.
- To present to people capable of critiquing.
- To be of service to the world."[18]

Not only does this hierarchy take the focus off of the teacher as the audience for learning but the higher up this hierarchy a student goes the more significant their motivation and engagement will be.[19] According to Berger et al., the highest audience would be for students to present their work as a service in the world.[20] Although teacher preparations are needed for effective classroom experiences, the voices and work of our students are essential to rich learning.

God has blessed us with cultural power with which we have an influence both in our classrooms and our communities. Each of us has been called to a different place and purpose to use the cultural power he has given us. Whether we use our cultural power intentionally or inadvertently, we are responsible for culture-making.

---

18. Berger et al., *Leaders of Their Own Learning*, 216.
19. Berger et al., *Leaders of Their Own Learning*, 215.
20. Berger et al., *Leaders of Their Own Learning*, 216.

TOGETHER

Name

Identifying Our Values[21]

STEP 1

Consider what values are most important to you. Consider using the table of values in table 2.[22] Choose two values that are most important to you. As this may be difficult on your first reading of the values list, consider circling about ten to begin with and then decide which of those two are the most important to you. (You may ask participants to complete this activity prior to meeting together.)

STEP 2

Consider the following questions to help you identify what your values look like in your day-to-day life:

1. What are three specific actions or habits that reflect and uphold each of my core values?
2. What kinds of behaviors or choices go against the values I hold most deeply?
3. Can I recall a time when I truly embodied each of these values? What did that look and feel like in practice?[23]

---

21. This activity was developed by Brené Brown as described in her book *Dare to Lead*.
22. This list was developed for educational reflection and includes values drawn from a variety of sources, including Brené Brown's published work on values in her book *Dare to Lead*.
23. Brown, *Dare to Lead*, 193.

Table 2
Identifying Our Values

Acceptance	Forgiveness	Love
Ambition	Forthright	Loyalty
Appreciation	Friendliness	Modesty
Benevolence	Fun-loving	Nurturing
Calmness	Generosity	Openness
Capable	Gentleness	Organization
Caring	Genuine	Passion
Cheerfulness	Giving	Patience
Clever	Goodness	Peace
Collaboration	Graciousness	Perceptive
Commitment	Gratefulness	Persistence
Community	Hardworking	Playfulness
Compassion	Helpful	Punctuality
Competence	Honesty	Reliability
Confidence	Humility	Resilience
Conscientiousness	Humor	Self-Aware
Considerate	Imagination	Self-Control
Courage	Incisiveness	Shrewd
Creativity	Inclusion	Spontaneity
Curiosity	Independence	Stability
Decisive	Insightful	Steadfast
Dependability	Innovation	Stewardship
Discipline	Integrity	Strength
Eloquence	Intuition	Tact
Empathy	Joyfulness	Teamwork
Encouragement	Justice	Thorough
Enthusiasm	Kindness	Tolerant
Equity	Knowledge	Trustworthiness
Fairness	Leadership	Understanding
Faithfulness	Learning	Vulnerability
Family	Listening	Wholeheartedness
Flexibility	Logical	Wisdom

Step 3

Answer these questions about both values you have chosen for yourself. (This too may be an activity where participants are asked to do this ahead of time in preparation for this session.)

Step 4

Have each person write their name on a piece of chart paper along with their two values. Gather in a circle and have each person name the one or two values they chose for themselves.

Game

Have each person write down one reason you appreciate that person and how they live into their values. (This may be done during one session, but preferably it is something that can be done over a week or two.)

Frame

Read "The Story of the Cracked Pot."

The Story of the Cracked Pot (Author Unknown)

A water bearer in India had two large pots, each hung on each end of a pole which he carried across his neck. One of the pots had a crack in it, and while the other pot was perfect and always delivered a full portion of water at the end of the long walk from the stream to the master's house, the cracked pot arrived only half full.

For a full two years, this went on daily, with the bearer delivering only one and a half pots full of water in his master's house. Of course, the perfect pot was proud of its accomplishments, perfect to the end for which it was made. But the poor cracked pot was ashamed of its own imperfection and miserable that it was able to accomplish only half of what it had been made to do.

After two years of what it perceived to be a bitter failure, it spoke to the water bearer one day by the stream. "I am ashamed of myself, and I want to apologize to you."

The bearer asked, "Why? What are you ashamed of?"

The pot replied, "For these past two years I am able to deliver only half of my load because this crack in my side causes water to leak out all the way back to your master's house. Because of my flaws, you don't get full value for your efforts."

The water bearer felt sorry for the old cracked pot, and in his compassion, he said, "As we return to the master's house, I want you to notice the beautiful flowers along the path."

As they went up the hill, the old cracked pot took notice of the sun warming the beautiful wildflowers on the side of the path, and this cheered it somewhat. But at the end of the trail, it still felt bad because it had leaked out half its load, and so again it apologized to the bearer for its failure.

The bearer said to the pot, "Did you notice that there were flowers only on your side of your path, but not on the other pot's side? That's because I have always known about your flaw, and I took advantage of it. I planted flower seeds on your side of the path, and every day while we walk back from the stream, you've watered them. For two years I have been able to pick these beautiful flowers to decorate my master's table. Without you being just the way you are, he would not have this beauty to grace his house."

GUIDING QUESTIONS

- Break into small groups of three and ask one person in each group to guide the conversation.
- Take turns sharing one quote from the chapter that stood out to you. Explain why it resonated with you personally or professionally.

- Use the questions provided below as conversation prompts. There is no need to answer every question—let them serve as starting points to spark meaningful discussion.
- After the discussion time ends, come back together as a full group. Invite each small group to share one key insight or meaningful moment from their conversation.

On Christian Teaching and *Ubuntu*

1. How does the concept of *Ubuntu*, "I am because we are," challenge or enhance your understanding of the classroom community?
2. Reflect on a time when collaboration with your colleagues or students enhanced the outcome for everyone involved. How does this align with *Ubuntu*?

Image-Bearing and Community

3. What does it mean to you to be created in the image of God, and how should this understanding shape the way we approach education?
4. How can teachers balance nurturing individual student growth while also fostering a strong sense of community within the classroom?
5. In what ways do your school's or classroom's practices currently celebrate students as God's image-bearers? What could be improved?

Christian Deeper Learning

6. How does Christian Deeper Learning differ from traditional approaches to education? Have you experienced or implemented deeper learning in your own educational context?
7. How can we ensure that group projects or collaborative activities genuinely build interpersonal skills rather than just focusing on academic outcomes?
8. What are some practical ways to incorporate "real work for real people with real needs" into the curriculum?

Global Citizenship and Impact

9. What role does education play in preparing students to be global citizens who seek justice and care for creation?
10. Share an example of a project or activity in your school that connected student learning with real-world issues or community impact. What made it successful?
11. How does connecting student work to a broader audience, as outlined in Berger's hierarchy, increase engagement and motivation?

8

Cultivating a Community of Learners

When we are fully able to bear the beauty of God resting upon us, when our work and worship are one, we will live in the eternal now of creators in the Creator's image.

—ANDY CROUCH

KINTSUGI: PUTTING BROKEN PIECES TOGETHER[1]

THERE IS A STORY told of an emperor in Japan who broke his favorite bowl. He sent it back to China, where it had originally been made, to have it repaired. When it was returned, it was full of ugly staples that held it together. The emperor called on the artists in his own country to devise a better solution for repairing his bowl, and so began the Japanese art of mending ceramics using gold seams. The process highlights the fact that the ceramic piece was broken by highlighting the cracks with golden veins, such that the history

---

1. van der Boom, "Kintsugi."

of brokenness makes the bowl more beautiful than it was before.[2] The brokenness represents essential moments in history. The flaws are not hidden but rather are celebrated.

How can we use this concept of redemption, the idea of turning broken pieces into objects more beautiful than the original, within the work of the classroom? I grew up with the desire to "change the world." Specifically, I wanted the education system to be better for students than it was for me. The reality is that we cannot change what already is, but we can play a part in transforming the world.

When I think back to my childhood, I recall how I struggled as a student and yet, by the grace of God, made it through my studies. As I was finishing my high school studies, I decided to become a teacher to help others navigate their own educational journey. I am the teacher I am today because of the brokenness that I experienced as a student. My philosophy of education is rooted in the belief that each student is uniquely created by God and that education should celebrate both diversity and community. Learning should be an experience that brings joy and a sense of belonging for all students in a class that integrates academic and social-emotional learning.

On a day-to-day basis I need to make decisions about how I interact with others and with creation. My decisions can either support God's restorative work or they can work against it. Supporting God's restorative work includes listening to others and becoming conscious of my own biases. It involves real work for real people as a response to loving God and loving others. It includes caring for the world by making decisions that look beyond my own conveniences and consider the value of the world's resources we have been entrusted with. I am challenged as an educator to continue to ask myself, "How does this contribute to God's restorative work?"

I love the reference to kintsugi, the art form that highlights the brokenness of a piece of pottery in such a way that this brokenness creates an opportunity for beauty that was not there before. Within education, we know that learning from mistakes is a

2. Winner, "Characteristic Damage," 8.

powerful learning opportunity. I wonder if talking about our mistakes or perhaps struggles is something that we don't do enough. As we face our own struggles and the struggles of our students, it is good to be reminded that even though God is the potter and we are the clay (Isa 64:8), he is also able to redeem our brokenness and make us beautiful.

BECOMING A CRITICALLY REFLECTIVE TEACHER

As an educator, I think a lot about pedagogy—what I will teach and how I will teach it. During the past number of years, I have thought more about whether my teaching practices are supporting the learning communities of belonging that I desire my classes to be. I wonder what my unconscious biases are and how I can teach in a way that truly celebrates each learner in my classroom. What are my assumptions about race and racism, human sexuality, and indigenous perspectives? Critical reflection according to Freire is more than thinking about one's practice; it includes action.[3]

Critically reflective teaching occurs when we identify and carefully consider the assumptions that shape our practice. Brookfield suggests that reflection becomes critical when it focuses on a teacher's understanding of power and hegemony.[4] By power it advises teachers to question the assumptions they have about the power dynamics of their classrooms and how they are using their power as a teacher. The concept of hegemony involves shaping the beliefs, values, and norms of society in such a way that the dominance of the ruling group appears natural and legitimate. This cultural dominance is achieved through institutions such as media, religion, and education.

As educators, we need to examine how our current practice may be supporting a class culture that is causing harm. Critically reflective teaching should consider common sense assumptions

---

3. Freire, *Pedagogy of the Oppressed*, 66.
4. Brookfield, *Becoming a Critically Reflective Teacher*, 9.

about what good teaching looks like. Assuming that our carefully planned classroom protocols will be experienced by each student in the same way is problematic.[5]

To transform teaching practices so that they lead to flourishing, I suggest using critical reflection. Critically reflective teaching occurs when we identify and carefully consider the assumptions that shape our practice. We desire to uncover unjust systems that are currently regarded as standard in the practice of education. Critically reflecting on our practice for justice guides us to focus on two kinds of assumptions: "(1) assumptions about power dynamics and what constitutes a justifiable exercise or abuse of power and (2) assumptions that seem common sense and serve us well but that actually work against our best interests (what are called hegemonic assumptions)."[6] The concept of hegemony is defined as "the process whereby ideas, structures, and actions that benefit a small minority in power are viewed by the majority of people as wholly natural, preordained, and working for their own good."[7] Therefore, reflection becomes critical when it focuses on an educator's understanding of power and hegemony, and their impact on pedagogical practice. Educators need to question their assumptions about the power dynamics within their classrooms and how they use their power as teachers. In society, hegemony stops people from challenging the status quo, so we need to examine how our current practices may be supporting a class culture that is causing harm, marginalizing, and oppressing.[8]

In his book *Becoming a Critically Reflective Teacher*, Stephen Brookfield suggests four necessary lenses to consider when critically reflecting on one's practice: students' eyes, colleagues' perceptions, personal experiences, and theory and research.[9] Students' learning experiences are diverse, and they interpret the educator's words and actions from their own context. Seeing ourselves

5. Brookfield, *Becoming a Critically Reflective Teacher*, 36.
6. Brookfield, *Becoming a Critically Reflective Teacher*, ix.
7. Brookfield, *Becoming a Critically Reflective Teacher*, 16.
8. Brookfield, *Becoming a Critically Reflective Teacher*, 39–40.
9. Brookfield, *Becoming a Critically Reflective Teacher*, 59.

through our students' eyes is one of the best ways to uncover the power dynamics in our classrooms and recognize hegemony. Teachers need to take the time to ask students to describe problems as they experience them in the classroom. Critical reflection is best practiced collaboratively by colleagues who often share many of the same or similar classroom experiences. They can help us reflect on how we have perceived things, challenge the assumptions we hold, and recognize the power dynamics in our classroom. We must work on becoming much more aware of the need to be conscious of microaggressions committed in groups of mixed-race, mixed-gender, or mixed-class classrooms and push back against practices that support racism, sexism, and classism. Personal experiences can have the most influential role in teaching, yet we often pay the least attention to this lens of critical reflection. As educators, we tend to repeat learning experiences that we felt were enriching and work to avoid learning experiences that we found boring or unhelpful. Theory tends to be the most challenging lens for educators to use as many classroom teachers have limited time to read and research educational theories. We all have access to each of these lenses, yet we do not use them equally due to external constraints, of which time is the most common.

Critical reflection is often used as a process for problem-solving. The idea of not trying to fix something that isn't broken may seem to make sense, but that is not the stance we want to take as teachers. As lifelong learners, critical reflection sets us up for a stance of ongoing inquiry and informed actions. Uncovering one's assumptions is part of being a good teacher as it helps us make informed decisions, develop a rationale for practice, and survive the emotional ups and downs that come with teaching.

A GROWTH MINDSET

A growth mindset is crucial in our efforts to cultivate learning communities of belonging, I recognize that applying it to the practice of listening and learning from others is not something I always prioritize. In his book *The 7 Habits of Highly Effective*

People, Stephen Covey emphasizes the importance of seeking to understand rather than being understood, which is a vital first step on our journey toward justice and true community.[10] I can learn from those who possess a fuller and more holistic understanding of Christ's redemption. This approach does not diminish my own culture; rather, it fosters covenantal relationships that enhance my understanding of my identity as a bearer of Christ's image more fully.

I know that we are always learning, but I continue to be amazed at how much I still need to learn about Christian education, even though I have spent most of my life as either a student or teacher in Christian education. Even when I was teaching in public schools, I was working out what it meant to teach as a Christian teacher. Over the last number of years, I have become more aware of the importance of learning together with my students. Education is not meant to be a dumping of information from one person onto another, but rather it is more like lighting a fire under each student such that they fulfill their own calling in the world. The idea of imagining in Christian ways encourages us to engage first in what God values and then see how we might use the resources in education to build those values into our students. I am reminded of the work of those in Christian Deeper Learning who ask themselves what it means to approach learning as participation in "God's Story."

BRINGING OUT THE BEST IN STUDENTS

Over the past fifty years, Finland's education system has improved significantly, resulting in students consistently exceeding expectations on PISA test scores. A popular mantra in Finnish schools is "We can't afford to waste a brain." This ethos sets their educational culture apart from other countries around the world. They understand that the key to nurturing hidden potential is not to invest

---

10. Covey, *7 Habits of Highly Effective People*, 146.

solely in students who show early signs of high ability, but to invest in every student, regardless of their apparent ability.[11]

Our school experiences can either fuel or hinder our growth. Some schools and teachers, despite limited resources, manage to create learning environments that bring out the best in us. Evidence from around the world shows that whether children thrive or struggle depends in part on the cultures created in schools and classrooms.[12]

According to organizational psychology, culture consists of three interconnected elements: practices, values, and underlying assumptions.[13] Practices are the daily routines that reflect and reinforce values. Values are shared beliefs about what is important or desirable. Underlying assumptions are the often unspoken, deeply held beliefs about how the world works—these shape our values, which in turn drive our practices.

Edgar Schein illustrates this complexity through his model of the Three Levels of Culture.[14] This model is frequently represented by the iceberg metaphor, in which observable practices appear above the surface, underlying values lie just below, and deeply held, often unexamined assumptions form the broad foundation beneath.

At the same time, practices can shape values and assumptions, not just express them. Philosopher James K. A. Smith argues that our desires are not formed only by what we believe but by the habits and practices we participate in—what he calls liturgies.[15] These daily rituals, both sacred and secular, shape our loves. According to Smith, the primary challenge to Christian education is not public schooling, but the powerful cultural practices—secular liturgies—that subtly train students to love things other than God. These practices do not merely reflect belief; they form it, guiding our hearts toward or away from God's ultimate love.

11. Grant, *Hidden Potential*, 134.
12. Grant, *Hidden Potential*, 134.
13. Grant, *Hidden Potential*, 134.
14. Schein and Schein, *Organizational Culture and Leadership*, 18.
15. J. K. A. Smith, "Higher Education."

Cultivating Learning Communities of Belonging

In table 3, competitive learning environments are contrasted with learning communities of belonging. The assumptions underlying each of these classroom cultures differ significantly: competitive classrooms may assume that some students are inherently smarter than others, whereas learning communities of belonging view each student as an image-bearer of God, with no student considered superior to another.

Competitive classrooms value the pursuit of excellence, often resulting in academically achieving students receiving special attention from teachers to further their growth opportunities. In contrast, students in learning communities of belonging focus on equity and belonging for all. The practices in the classroom encourage students to share their thoughts and be heard, emphasizing the importance of relationships in the learning process.

Table 3

Cultures in Education

Competitive Learning Environments[16]	Model of Culture[17]	Learning Communities of Belonging
Some students are smarter than others.	Assumptions Our beliefs about how the world works.	All students are image-bearers of God.
Achieving excellence	Values Shared principles about what is important and desirable.	Equity and belonging for all
Top students get top teachers and special attention.	Practices Daily routines that are visible or audible in the classroom.	Each student's voice is heard each day. Relationships are vital to learning.

Finland's education system has fostered a culture of opportunity for all students. Educators and school leaders believe that intelligence manifests in many forms and every child has the potential

---

16. Grant, *Hidden Potential*, 160.
17. Schein and Schein, *Organizational Culture and Leadership*, 18.

to excel. This belief underpins a central value of educational equity and drives practices designed to help every child succeed. Success is not exclusively reserved for the gifted and talented but strives to provide all students with excellent teachers and a personalized learning plan. The focus is on nurturing each student's interests, not solely on promoting their academic success.[18]

CULTIVATORS AND CREATORS

Culture can be so much richer if we focus on God's story in which we have roles as culture keepers and makers.[19] The idea that "creation begins with cultivation" is an important beginning step in living out our calling as people of God's story that shapes the world as we learn to take care of the good things that we already find in culture.[20] Cultivating requires careful attention to history and current events. Small and seemingly insignificant disciplines can have powerful cultural effects. So, together with culture-making, we find ourselves also culture-keeping—we are both creators and cultivators.

In 1 Cor 12:12-14, we read about one body with many parts:

> [12] For just as the body is one and has many members, and all the members of the body, though many, are one body, so it is with Christ. [13] For in the one Spirit we were all baptized into one body—Jews or Greeks, slaves or free—and we were all made to drink of one Spirit. [14] Indeed, the body does not consist of one member but of many.

God intentionally made us different from one another so that we could rely on each other and grow together.

---

18. Grant, *Hidden Potential*, 159.
19. Crouch, *Culture Making*, 74-75.
20. Crouch, *Culture Making*, 74.

TOGETHER

Name

Sit or stand in a circle. Go around and share one *joy* and one *challenge* you are currently experiencing. This may be from your personal life, professional life, or a combination of both. If you have a large group, consider asking participants to limit their *joy* and *challenge* to one sentence.

Game

"One Word" is an activity where participants share one word about each other's personalities. Begin by giving each participant a sheet of paper, a thin-tipped marker, and a piece of tape. Instruct everyone to write their name in the center of their paper and then tape it on the wall or window around the room, forming a large circle. (Alternatively, this can be done around a circle of desks or tables.)

Next, ask everyone to walk clockwise around the room, stopping at each piece of paper with someone's name on it. Quickly, they should think of one word that captures an important aspect of that person's personality (e.g., wise, kind, thoughtful) and write it on their respective paper. Encourage them not to look at what others have written.

Once each person has added one word to every page, they should end up in front of their own paper, now filled with words that describe them from their colleagues' perspectives.

Frame

Read Ps 90:14–17:

> 14 Satisfy us in the morning with your steadfast love,
>   so that we may rejoice and be glad all our days.
> 15 Make us glad as many days as you have afflicted us
>   and as many years as we have seen evil.
> 16 Let your work be manifest to your servants

and your glorious power to their children.
17 Let the favor of the Lord our God be upon us
and prosper for us the work of our hands—
O prosper the work of our hands!

GUIDING QUESTIONS

- Break into small groups of three and ask one person in each group to guide the conversation.
- Take turns sharing one quote from the chapter that stood out to you. Explain why it resonated with you personally or professionally.
- Use the questions provided below as conversation prompts. There is no need to answer every question—let them serve as starting points to spark meaningful discussion.
- After the discussion time ends, come back together as a full group. Invite each small group to share one key insight or meaningful moment from their conversation.

On Brokenness and Restoration

1. How does the art of kintsugi reflect the idea of restoration in education? Can you think of a time when a challenge or mistake in the classroom led to growth or unexpected beauty?
2. What steps can educators take to help students see their struggles or failures as opportunities for growth rather than setbacks?

Cultivating a Learning Community

3. The chapter highlights the importance of creating "learning communities of belonging." What specific practices can foster such an environment, especially in diverse classrooms?
4. How can acknowledging our biases, as the chapter suggests, impact the inclusiveness of classroom culture?

Critical Reflection in Teaching

5. The chapter emphasizes critical reflection as a way to address assumptions about power dynamics and hegemony. What tools or practices have you found helpful for engaging in this kind of reflection as a teacher?
6. How might a critically reflective approach to teaching impact relationships with students and colleagues?

Growth Mindset and Deeper Learning

7. What does applying a growth mindset to listening and learning from others look like in practice? How can this approach contribute to building a justice-oriented classroom?
8. How does deeper learning, as described in the chapter, align with the goals of Christian education? What practices could bring this approach to life in your teaching?

Culture in Education

9. The chapter contrasts competitive learning environments with communities of belonging. How can educators shift

classroom culture to value relationships over competition while still promoting excellence?

10. How does the Finnish model of education, with its emphasis on equity and personalized learning, challenge the practices in your own educational context?

Celebrating Diversity and Unity

11. The chapter reflects on the importance of celebrating differences within the body of Christ. How can teachers incorporate this principle into their pedagogy while addressing cultural or systemic inequities?

12. What role does storytelling (e.g., God's story or students' personal narratives) play in cultivating a culture of belonging and growth in the classroom?

9

Hospitable Classrooms

Instead of an object to be evangelized, a stranger to be avoided, a sympathy case to be donated to, all of which involve an unequal power relationship, hospitality, when performed as a biblical practice, transforms the Other into someone to be learned from, someone to be invited in, someone to be in relationship with.

—Aminta Arrington

WHAT MIGHT CHRISTIAN EDUCATION LOOK LIKE?

What might Christian schools and classrooms look like if we invited our neighbors in—not in a way in which our differences create a hierarchy, but one in which we can learn from one another? Fourth-grade students at Halton Hills Christian School in Georgetown, Ontario, Canada, did just that. In March 2019, after the mosque shootings in Christchurch, New Zealand, one of the students asked, "Why did those gunmen want to shoot those people in New Zealand? I bet if they only knew some Muslim people, they wouldn't want to hurt them. They could be friends instead."[1]

This question sparked a meaningful classroom discussion, during which many students realized they had never met a Muslim peer. That year, the school's guiding question was "What does love require?"—a call that demanded courageous action. With support from school leadership, the teacher reached out to a nearby Muslim school to propose a shared day of learning. The Muslim school was delighted with the invitation as they also wanted to break down barriers and increase their students' understanding of others.[2] Their day together was a wonderful success as the students played games such as "Just Like Me" in which they found many similarities with one another. Students, teachers, and school administrators found that they had more in common than they had differences with one another. This is an illustration of how engaging students in authentic and purposeful interactions with their neighbors is one way to show love and hospitality.

Hospitality is often understood as a warm and generous way of welcoming and caring for others, including guests, visitors, and those who may be unfamiliar or new. When we think of hospitality, we often consider sharing food, drinks, accommodation, and entertainment. Pedagogical hospitality involves teachers embracing the vulnerability of welcoming their students and their stories. This is why educators must dedicate time to truly get to know their students and be willing to humbly adjust their lessons to meet their students' needs better.[3]

Hospitality as such creates a space in which we make ourselves available to help one another and show gratitude for the gift of hospitality we receive from each other. As Christians, the culture of hospitality should come from a belief that every person is an image-bearer of God. In her paper "Becoming a World Christian: Hospitality as a Framework for Engaging Otherness," Aminta Arrington describes true Christian hospitality as "the

1. Vangoor, "What Does Love Require?"
2. Vangoor, "What Does Love Require?"
3. Chalwell, "You Are Welcome," 221.

acknowledgment of the image of God in every person, and the desire to have eyes that see that individual's needs."[4] Thought from an assistance mindset, hospitality includes hierarchy, inequality, and differences, and often leads to paternalism, patronizing superiority, and even discrimination.[5]

Students arrive at school with physical, mental, and emotional needs—not just academic needs. A welcoming teacher recognizes and acknowledges those needs even though the school or teacher may not be able to meet them.[6] The hospitality we want to be practiced in Christian schools allows needs to be expressed rather than dismissed or ignored, and "cultivates empathy, embodies reciprocity, and leads to transformation."[7] This transformation allows us to see everyone as worthy of being invited in, learned from, and in a relationship with.[8]

Arrington tells the story of some university students volunteering at a center for children with special needs. Instead of framing the interaction between the students as one in which the university students are helping the children with special needs, she explains how the encounter is one of hospitality.[9] Contrary to the common understanding of this type of interaction as one in which the volunteers host the children with special needs, the latter host the former.

FLOURISHING COMMUNITY AND JUST RELATIONSHIPS

In his book *Culture Making: Recovering Our Creative Calling*, Andy Crouch challenges us to consider whether we have been

---

4. Arrington, "Becoming a World Christian," 27.
5. Arrington, "Becoming a World Christian," 27.
6. Lepp-Kaethler and Rust-Akinbolaji, "Welcoming the Guest," 220.
7. Arrington, "Becoming a World Christian," 29.
8. Arrington, "Becoming a World Christian," 36.
9. Arrington, "Becoming a World Christian," 26–27.

called to change the world or to transform culture.[10] He suggests we should take culture as it is and create more of it. Crouch writes, "So if we seek to change culture, we will have to create something new, something that will persuade our neighbors to set aside some existing set of cultural goods for our new proposal."[11] Proper understanding of a person or a cultural good requires participation—such as seeking opportunities for collaboration between the Christian school and other schools in the area. Joint educational programs, sports events, or cultural exchanges foster a sense of unity and break down stereotypes.

Klingenstein Teacher Award Finalist for 2021 Shatera Weaver paints a picture of how she creates an affirming space for identity and belonging at school. Rather than planning how to create a culture of belonging for her students, she prefers to explore ways to co-create classroom cultures with them. Many students, she says, feel defeated and have to ask for help, but when they have the opportunity to celebrate and recognize themselves, their fear tends to dwindle. We need to continue to work toward creating classroom cultures that establish flourishing communities and just relationships.

God has blessed us with cultural power with which we have an influence both in our classrooms and our communities. Each of us has been called to a different place and purpose to use the cultural power he has given us. Whether we use our cultural power intentionally or inadvertently, we are responsible for culture-making.

CREATING CLASSROOMS OF HOSPITALITY AND RESPECT

Classrooms must become places where students and teachers treat each other as guests, with hospitality and respect. This approach fosters a welcoming and inclusive environment where everyone feels valued and heard. Here are some ways to cultivate hospitality and respect in the classroom:

10. Crouch, *Culture Making*, 67.
11. Crouch, *Culture Making*, 67.

1. Welcoming Atmosphere: Create a physical and emotional environment that feels safe and welcoming for all students. Decorate the classroom with diverse representations and encourage open dialogue.
2. Respectful Interactions: Model and enforce respectful interactions among students and between students and teachers. This includes active listening, kindness, and empathy in all communications.
3. Inclusive Curriculum: Incorporate diverse perspectives and voices into the curriculum. Ensure that all students see themselves reflected in the materials and that their experiences are validated.
4. Community Engagement: Encourage students to engage with people in their communities. This can be done through projects, partnerships, and service learning that emphasize hospitality and deeper learning.
5. Christian Deeper Learning Practices: Promote practices of Christian Deeper Learning that go beyond surface-level understanding. This involves critical thinking, collaboration, and real-world problem-solving, which can be enriched through community involvement and hospitality.

By treating each other with hospitality and respect in our classrooms and engaging with our communities through deeper learning, we can contribute to meaningful change in our schools, communities, and beyond.

COMMUNITIES OF BELONGING

Trees in a forest can be thought of as fierce competitors, each struggling to reach up and access sunlight from above and moisture in the soil below. And yet, there is research that shows that trees practice reciprocity and value diversity. Simard et al. have found that birch trees help nearby Douglas-firs by transferring carbon (sugar) through underground strands of beneficial fungi called ectomycorrhiza.[12] In a symbiotic relationship, the fungus obtains carbohydrates and vitamins from the tree, increasing the absorptive surface of the root, and allowing an increase in water and essential elements to be taken in by the tree. When birch trees are removed from growing with conifers, they lose their vigor and die within a few years. The birch only flourishes in communities with trees that are different from themselves. What a beautiful symbol of community unity with individual diversity.

TOGETHER

Name

Tell a story about your name. Who gave it to you? Are you named after someone? Do you have a nickname?

Game

Play a game of "Just Like Me." Begin by sitting or standing a group in a circle where they can see and hear one another.

Tell the group that the goal of the game is to discover things we have in common. When someone shares something true about themselves, others who share that trait or experience will respond by saying, "Just like me!"

One person starts and says something about themselves. E.g., "I like to eat ice cream." "I have a little brother." "I'm scared of spiders." "I wear glasses." "I speak more than one language." Anyone in the circle who identifies with that statement responds enthusiastically: "Just like me!" You can also encourage participants to take a small step forward or raise a hand when saying it.

Either go in order around the circle or let volunteers take turns. Ensure everyone has a chance to speak.

---

12. Simard et al., "Net Transfer of Carbon," 580.

Frame

Going around the circle, share one way you experience belonging in your school or classroom.

GUIDING QUESTIONS

- Break into small groups of three and ask one person in each group to guide the conversation.
- Take turns sharing one quote from the chapter that stood out to you. Explain why it resonated with you personally or professionally.
- Use the questions provided below as conversation prompts. There is no need to answer every question—let them serve as starting points to spark meaningful discussion.
- After the discussion time ends, come back together as a full group. Invite each small group to share one key insight or meaningful moment from their conversation.

Understanding Hospitality in Education

1. How does the biblical practice of hospitality differ from the commonly held notion of helping others?
2. What does it mean to transform "the Other" into someone to learn from, rather than someone to pity or avoid?
3. Can you share an example from your own experience where hospitality in a classroom led to deeper understanding and relationships?

Practical Applications

4. In what ways can educators create spaces for students to share their stories and experiences authentically?
5. How can Christian schools and teachers engage with their local communities to foster reciprocal learning and respect?
6. What challenges might arise when trying to create hospitable classrooms, and how can they be addressed?

Community and Interdependence

7. What lessons can we learn from nature, such as the interconnection between birch and Douglas-fir trees, about building interdependent classroom communities?
8. How can classroom cultures promote flourishing communities where every individual feels valued and supported?
9. What does co-creating classroom culture with students look like in practice?

Theological and Philosophical Reflections

10. How does acknowledging every student as an image-bearer of God influence classroom dynamics and teaching practices?
11. How can Christian educators balance their cultural power to ensure it is used for justice and restoration rather than hierarchy or exclusion?

Building Inclusive and Just Classrooms

12. What are some steps teachers can take to create a welcoming and inclusive environment for diverse student populations?
13. How can anti-racist and inclusive practices be integrated into everyday teaching?
14. How does creating "communities of belonging" align with the Christian mission of restoration and justice?

CLOSING CIRCLE

Have participants stand in a large circle. Take a ball of yarn and pass it from one participant to the other with each participant hanging on to the piece of yarn in front of them. Once everyone is holding a piece of yarn, read the following script:

Imagine with me that we are in a forest. Let's imagine we are in the forest of giant sequoia trees on this particular day. Our circle of bodies surrounds just one of these trees. The tree measures 31 meters in circumference at its base and has a diameter of 9 meters.

The giant sequoia trees growing in California have a beautiful story of unity to share. These incredible trees can live up to 3,000 years. They have branches up to 2.5 meters in diameter. Their bark can grow up to almost one meter thick. When you look up, you notice that the largest of the sequoias are as tall as an average 26-story building.[13]

One would imagine that supporting that size and weight would require deep roots. The roots of a giant sequoia are relatively shallow as they grow only 1.8 to 6 meters below the soil. Rarely, however, do these great trees fall over. The secret to the strength of the sequoia giants is that they function as a community. Now, imagine with me that the yarn you are holding is a piece of that root system. Each tree is dependent on the other trees around it as their roots are intertwined. It is their dense network that shares support

---

13. Breyer, "16 Spectacular Facts About Giant Sequoias."

and nutrients which provides incredible strength and stability to these giant trees. These trees grow very close together and they hold each other up.[14] It is because of their intertwined root systems that they can stand firm against wind, fire, earthquakes, and storms.[15]

God has created us, as the giant sequoia trees, to intertwine our root systems to support one another.

Keep holding the root you have in front of you. I will come around and cut it so that you can take it with you as a reminder of our time together. You are not alone. Your roots are intertwined so that you can weather the storms that come your way.

Go around the circle and cut the yarn between each person. Encourage participants to tie this around their wrist or somewhere meaningful so that they will remember they are part of a large root system that supports each other.

A Final Blessing

> Go in peace as you love and serve the Lord—
> not alone
> but with your roots intertwined
> so that you will be able to weather the storms
> that come your way.

---

14. Williamson, "What Kind of Root System Do You Have?," para. 4.
15. Eckert, *Just Teaching*, 27.

Bibliography

American Psychological Association Zero Tolerance Task Force. "Are Zero Tolerance Policies Effective in the Schools? An Evidentiary Review and Recommendations." *American Psychologist* 63 (2008) 852–62.

Amosu, Oluwabunmi. "Green Disciples: Sustainability Starts with Each of Us." EduDeo Ministries, April 21, 2024. https://edudeo.com/news/2024/04/21/green-disciples.

Arrington, Aminta. "Becoming a World Christian: Hospitality as a Framework for Engaging Otherness." *International Journal of Christianity and Education* 21 (2017) 26–38.

Barkaskas, Patricia, and Derek Gladwin. "Pedagogical Talking Circles: Decolonizing Education Through Relational Indigenous Frameworks." *Journal of Teaching and Learning* 15 (2021) 20–38.

BC Human Rights Commission. "Decolonization." https://bchumanrights.ca/key-issues/decolonization/.

Berger, Ron, et al. *Leaders of Their Own Learning: Transforming Schools Through Student-Engaged Assessment*. San Francisco: Jossey-Bass, 2014.

Breyer, Mary. "16 Spectacular Facts About Giant Sequoias." *Treehugger*, 2021. https://www.treehugger.com/spectacular-facts-about-giant-sequoias-4858757.

Brookfield, Stephen. *Becoming a Critically Reflective Teacher*. 2nd ed. San Francisco: Jossey-Bass, 2017.

Brown, Brené. *Dare to Lead: Brave Work. Tough Conversations. Whole Hearts.* New York: Random House, 2018.

Brummer, Joe. *Building a Trauma-Informed Restorative School: Skills and Approaches for Improving Culture and Behavior*. London: Jessica Kingsley, 2020.

Bruner, Jerome. *Acts of Meaning: Four Lectures on Mind and Culture*. Cambridge, MA: Harvard University Press, 1990.

Burdick, Lynn S., and Catherine Corr. "Helping Teachers Understand and Mitigate Trauma in Their Classrooms." *Teaching Exceptional Children* 53 (2021) 250–58.

BIBLIOGRAPHY

Carleton, Sean. *Lessons in Legitimacy: Colonialism, Capitalism, and the Rise of State Schooling in British Columbia.* Vancouver: University of British Columbia Press, 2022.

Chalwell, Kaye. "You Are Welcome: Hospitality Encounters in Teaching." In *Reimagining Christian Education: Cultivating Transformative Approaches,* edited by Johannes M. Luetz et al., 209-32. New York: Springer, 2018.

Charles, Mark, and Soong-Chan Rah. *Unsettling Truths: The Ongoing Dehumanizing Legacy of the Doctrine of Discovery.* Downers Grove, IL: InterVarsity, 2019.

Chen, Michelle, et al. "From White to Mosaic." In *MindShift: Catalyzing Change in Christian Education,* edited by Lynn E. Swaner et al., 65-79. Colorado Springs: Association of Christian Schools International, 2019.

Christian Deeper Learning. "About Us." Christian Schools International. https://www.christiandeeperlearning.org/.

Chrona, Jo. *Wayi Wah! Indigenous Pedagogies: An Act for Reconciliation and Anti-Racist Education.* Winnipeg: Portage & Main, 2022.

Claro, Susana, et al. "Growth Mindset Tempers the Effects of Poverty on Academic Achievement." *Proceedings of the National Academy of Sciences* 113 (2016) 8664-68.

Cole, Susan F., et al. *Helping Traumatized Children Learn: Supportive School Environments for Children Traumatized by Family Violence.* Boston: Massachusetts Advocates for Children, Trauma and Learning Policy Initiative, 2009.

Cook, Justin, and Darryl DeBoer. "Deeper Learning in Christian Education: Deeper Learning into What?" *The Christian Teachers Journal* 26 (2018) 12-16.

Covey, Stephen R. *The 7 Habits of Highly Effective People: Powerful Lessons in Personal Change.* New York: Simon & Schuster, 1989.

Crouch, Andy. *Culture Making: Recovering Our Creative Calling.* Downers Grove, IL: InterVarsity, 2008.

———. *Strong and Weak: Embracing a Life of Love, Risk and True Flourishing.* Downers Grove, IL: InterVarsity, 2016.

Cummins, Jim. "Teaching Through a Multilingual Lens: Classroom Resources for Global Education." In *Inquiry into Practice: Learning and Teaching Global Matters in Local Classrooms,* edited by Dora Montemurro et al., 12-15. Toronto: Ontario Institute for Studies in Education (OISE), 2014.

De La Torre, Miguel A. *Reading the Bible from the Margins.* Maryknoll, NY: Orbis, 2002.

Dewey, John. *Experience and Education.* New York: Free Press, 1997.

Eckert, Jonathan. *Just Teaching: Feedback, Engagement, and Well-Being for Each Student.* Thousand Oaks, CA: Corwin, 2023.

Evans, Katherine, and Dorothy Vaandering. *The Little Book of Restorative Justice in Education: Fostering Responsibility, Healing, and Hope in Schools.* New York: Good Books, 2022.

Faith Alive Christian Resources. *Ecumenical Creeds and Reformed Confessions.* Grand Rapids: Faith Alive Christian Resources, 1988.

Farkas, Steve. "Canadian Decolonization: The Path to Indigenous Recognition and Sovereignty." *Canadian Journal of Practical Philosophy* 7 (2021) 1–16.

First Nations Education Steering Committee. *Principles of Learning First People.* Poster. 2008. https://www.fnesc.ca/first-peoples-principles-of-learning/.

Fisher, Doug, and Nancy Frey. "Restorative Practices: Circles in the Classroom." YouTube video, June 19, 2025. https://www.youtube.com/watch?v=ZxxZ9yuqy6Q.

———. "Restorative Practices: Students' Perspectives." YouTube video, June 19, 2025. https://www.youtube.com/watch?v=R_w-VY3Y7EU.

Freire, Paulo. *Pedagogy of the Oppressed.* New York: Bloomsbury Academic, 2018.

Gilbert, Louise, et al. *Emotion Coaching with Children and Young People in Schools: Promoting Positive Behavior, Wellbeing and Resilience.* London: Jessica Kingsley, 2021.

Giroux, Henry. *On Critical Pedagogy.* 2nd ed. New York: Bloomsbury Academic, 2020.

Goodenow, Carol. "Classroom Belonging Among Early Adolescent Students: Relationships to Motivation and Achievement." *The Journal of Early Adolescence* 13 (1993) 21–43.

Grant, Adam. *Hidden Potential: The Science of Achieving Greater Things.* New York: Viking, 2023.

Halladay Goldman, Jennifer, et al. *Trauma-Informed School Strategies During COVID-19.* National Child Traumatic Stress Network, 2020. https://www.nctsn.org/sites/default/files/resources/resource-guide/trauma_informed_school_strategies_during_covid-19.pdf.

Harvard Project Zero. "Circle of Viewpoints." Project Zero, Harvard Graduate School of Education. https://pz.harvard.edu/resources/circle-of-viewpoints.

Hatcher, Annamarie, et al. "Two-Eyed Seeing in the Classroom Environment: Concepts, Approaches, and Challenges." *Canadian Journal of Science, Mathematics and Technology Education* 9 (2009) 141–53.

Hekman, Brian. "Schools as Communities of Grace." *Christian Educators Journal*, 2013.

Hopkins, Belinda. "From Restorative Justice to Restorative Culture." *Revista de Asistență Socială* 4 (2015) 19–34.

Ibrahim, Andrew M. "Becoming Anti-Racist: Fear, Learning, Growth." X, June 6, 2020. https://x.com/AndrewMIbrahim/status/1269423199273525250.

Indigenous Services Canada. *Annual Report to Parliament 2020.* https://www.sac-isc.gc.ca/eng/1602010609492/1602010631711.

Joe, Mi'sel, et al. "Two-Eared Listening Is Essential for Understanding Restorative Justice in Canada." *The Canadian*, July 11, 2022. https://theconversation.com/two-eared-listening-is-essential-for-understanding-restorative-justice-in-canada-185466.

Joldersma, Clarence W. "Doing Justice Today: A Welcoming Embrace for LGBT Students in Christian Schools." *International Journal of Christianity and Education* 20 (2016) 32–48.

Joseph, Bob. *21 Things You May Not Know About the Indian Act: Helping Canadians Make Reconciliation with Indigenous Peoples a Reality*. Port Coquitlam, BC: Indigenous Relations Press, 2018.

Kim, Paul Y. "How a Pad-Mounted Transformer and Stair Spindle Help Me Teach About Racial Microaggressions." *Christian Scholar's Review*, April 23, 2021. https://christianscholars.com/guest-post-how-a-pad-mounted-transformer-and-stair-spindle-help-me-teach-about-racial-microaggressions/.

Kimmerer, Robin Wall. *Braiding Sweetgrass: Indigenous Wisdom, Scientific Knowledge, and the Teaching of Plants*. Minneapolis: Milkweed Editions, 2013.

Kits, Gerda J. "Why Educating for Shalom Requires Decolonization." *International Journal of Christianity and Education* 23 (2019) 185–203.

Leddy, Shannon, and Lisa Miller. *Teaching Where You Are: Weaving Indigenous and Slow Principles and Pedagogies*. Toronto: University of Toronto Press, 2024.

Lepp-Kaethler, Erin, and Christa Rust-Akinbolaji. "Welcoming the Guest: Approach, Design, Procedure for Hospitable Learning Communities." In *Christian Higher Education in Canada: Challenges and Opportunities*, edited by Stanley E. Porter and Bruce G. Fawcett, 209–32. Eugene, OR: Pickwick, 2020.

Lodi, Ernesto, et al. "Use of Restorative Justice and Restorative Practices at School: A Systematic Literature Review." *International Journal of Environmental Research and Public Health* 19 (2021) 1–34.

Loewen, David. "How Shall We Disagree?" *The Link* 46 (2023) 3–5.

Maslow, Abraham H. "A Theory of Human Motivation." *Psychological Review* 50 (1943) 370–96.

McVety, David. "Season 1—Ep. 2 | PLC Sexuality and Christian Education." Langley Christian School, aired October 25, 2021. https://www.youtube.com/watch?v=wPHVyBHJYIM.

Merriam-Webster, s.v. "Racism." Accessed March 3, 2025. https://www.merriam-webster.com/dictionary/racism.

Métis National Council. "Frequently Asked Questions." https://www.metisnation.ca/about/faq.

Miller, James Roger. *Residential Schools and Reconciliation: Canada Confronts Its History*. Toronto: University of Toronto Press, 2017.

Moore, Sylvia, et al. "Decolonization Through Two-Eared Listening: The Integral Role of Listening to Indigenous Community Voices and Stories." *EdCan Network*, January 26, 2023. https://www.edcan.ca/articles/decolonization-through-two-eared-listening/.

Morrison, Brenda, et al. "Practicing Restorative Justice in School Communities: Addressing the Challenge of Culture Change." *Public Organization Review* 5 (2005) 335–57.

Mouw, Richard J. *Abraham Kuyper: A Short and Personal Introduction.* Grand Rapids: Eerdmans, 2011.

National Centre for Truth and Reconciliation. "Residential Schools Memorial." Accessed April 1, 2025. https://nctr.ca/memorial/#.

National Child Traumatic Stress Network, Schools Committee. *Creating, Supporting, and Sustaining Trauma-Informed Schools: A System Framework.* Los Angeles: National Center for Child Traumatic Stress, 2017.

Newman, Carey. "Welcome to the Witness Blanket." Canadian Museum for Human Rights. YouTube video, June 6, 2022. https://www.youtube.com/watch?v=WmTUoW1SgCA.

Ng, Greer Anne Wai-In. "Complexities in Religious Education with Asian/Asian Canadians and Indigenous Realities: The Truth and Reconciliation Commission Report on Residential Schools." *Religious Education* 115 (2020) 315–22.

Osterman, Karen F. "Students' Need for Belonging in the School Community." *Review of Educational Research* 70 (2000) 323–67.

Peters, William, dir. "A Class Divided. Frontline." *PBS*, March 26, 1985. https://www.pbs.org/wgbh/frontline/documentary/class-divided/.

Prete, Tiffany, and Elizabeth Lange. "Indigenous Voices and Decolonising Lifelong Education." *International Journal of Lifelong Education* 40 (2021) 303–9.

Queen's University. "Definitions: Decolonizing and Indigenizing." https://www.queensu.ca/indigenous/decolonizing-and-indigenizing/definitions.

Ramsay, Nancy. "Teaching Effectively in Racially and Culturally Diverse Classrooms." *Teaching Theology and Religion* 8 (2005) 18–23.

Restorative Practice Consortium. *Restorative Practice Resource Project: Tools and Successful Practices for Restorative Schools Supporting Student Achievement and Well-Being.* 2017. https://restorative.ca/wp-content/uploads/2019/12/RESTORATIVE-PRACTICE-RESOURCE-PROJECT.pdf.

Robertson, John T. *Overlooked: The Forgotten Stories of Canadian Christianity.* Saskatoon, SK: New Leaf Network, 2022.

Robinson, Peter. "Acculturation, Enculturation, and Social Imaginaries: The Complex Relationship Between the Gospel and Culture." In *Decolonizing Discipline: Children, Corporal Punishment, Christian Theologies, and Reconciliation*, edited by V. Michaelson and J. E. Durrant, 67–76. Winnipeg: University of Manitoba Press, 2020.

Schein, Edgar H., and Peter A. Schein. *Organizational Culture and Leadership.* 5th ed. Hoboken, NJ: Wiley, 2017.

Simard, Suzanne, et al. "Net Transfer of Carbon Between Ectomycorrhizal Tree Species in the Field." *Nature* 388 (1997) 579–82.

Sinclair, Murray. "TRC Mini Documentary—Senator Murray Sinclair on Reconciliation." June 19, 2025. https://www.youtube.com/watch?v=wjx2z DvyzsU.
Sleeter, Christine. "Confronting the Marginalization of Culturally Responsive Pedagogy." *Urban Education* 47 (2012) 562–84.
Sloat, Savannah. "What Does Indigenization Mean?" *University Affairs*, April 3, 2024. https://universityaffairs.ca/opinion/what-does-indigenization-mean/.
Smith, David I. *On Christian Teaching: Practicing Faith in the Classroom*. Grand Rapids: Eerdmans, 2018.
Smith, David I., and Barbara Carville. *The Gift of the Stranger: Faith, Hospitality, and Foreign Language Learning*. Grand Rapids: Eerdmans, 2000.
Smith, James K. A. *Desiring the Kingdom: Worship, Worldview, and Cultural Formation*. Cultural Liturgies 1. Grand Rapids: Baker Academic, 2009.
———. "Higher Education: What's Love Got to Do with It? Longings, Desires and Human Flourishings." Keynote address at Learning and Loves: Reimagining Christian Education, CHC Higher Education Research Symposium, Brisbane, Australia, July 2016. https://youtu.be/TAg6sn4XJMc.
Smith, Julia. "SOGI Statements and LGBT+ Student Care in Christian Schools." *International Journal of Christianity and Education* 25 (2021) 290–309.
Souers, Kristin, and Pete Hall. *Fostering Resilient Learners: Strategies for Creating a Trauma-Sensitive Classroom*. Alexandria, VA: ASCD, 2016.
Spencer, Steven J., et al. "Stereotype Threat." *Annual Review of Psychology* 67 (2016) 415–37.
Sporleder, Jim, and Heather T. Forbes. *The Trauma-Informed School: A Step-by-Step Implementation Guide for Administrators and School Personnel*. Beyond Consequences Institute, 2016.
Tisby, Jemar. *How to Fight Racism: Courageous Christianity and the Journey Toward Racial Justice*. Grand Rapids: Zondervan Reflective, 2021.
Trauma Learning Policy Initiative. "How Can Trauma-Sensitive Schools Embrace Student Voice?" Helping Traumatized Children Learn, March 26, 2025. https://traumasensitiveschools.org/how-can-trauma-sensitive-schools-embrace-student-voice/.
Truth and Reconciliation Commission of Canada. *Canada's Residential Schools: Reconciliation*. Final Report of the Truth and Reconciliation Commission of Canada. Montreal: McGill-Queen's University Press, 2015.
———. *Honouring the Truth, Reconciling for the Future: Summary of the Final Report of the Truth and Reconciliation Commission of Canada*. 2015. https://irsi.ubc.ca/sites/default/files/inline-files/Executive_Summary_English_Web.pdf.
———. *What We Have Learned: Principles of Truth and Reconciliation*. 2015. https://ehprnh2mwo3.exactdn.com/wp-content/uploads/2021/01/Principles_English_Web.pdf.

Tulshyan, Ruchika. *Inclusion on Purpose: An Intersectional Approach to Creating a Culture of Belonging at Work*. Cambridge, MA: MIT Press, 2022.

UNESCO. *Education for People and Planet: Creating Sustainable Futures for All*. Global Education Monitoring Report. Paris: UNESCO, 2016.

van der Boom, Edith H. "Kintsugi: Putting Broken Pieces Together." Christian Deeper Learning, May 24, 2022. https://www.christiandeeperlearning.org/post/kintsugi-putting-broken-pieces-together.

———. "Ubuntu: I Am Because We Are." Christian Deeper Learning, April 17, 2022. https://www.christiandeeperlearning.org/post/ubuntu-i-am-because-we-are.

Van der Kolk, Bessel A. *The Body Keeps the Score: Brain, Mind, and Body in the Healing of Trauma*. New York: Penguin, 2015.

Vangoor, M. "What Does Love Require?" *ACSI Blog*, 2019. https://blog.acsi.org/love-thy-neighbor.

Volo, Mandisa. "Powerful Poetry About Racial Discrimination: Mandisa Volo's Winning Speech." YouTube video, March 7, 2019. https://www.youtube.com/watch?v=DalcpicHwVc.

Walton, Gregory M., and Geoffrey L. Cohen. "A Brief Social-Belonging Intervention Improves Academic and Health Outcomes of Minority Students." *Science* 331 (2011) 1447–51.

Williams, Jenny, and Amanda Broadway. "School as a Place of Healing and Hope for Students Impacted by Trauma." *The Link* 46 (2023) 3–5.

Williamson, Susan. "What Kind of Root System Do You Have?" Maxwell Leadership Certified Team. https://johnmaxwellteam.com/what-kind-of-root-system-do-you-have/.

Winner, Lauren F. "Characteristic Damage." In *The Dangers of Christian Practice: On Wayward Practice, Characteristic Damage, and Sin*, 1–18. New Haven, CT: Yale University Press, 2018.

Wolterstorff, Nicholas. *Education for Shalom: Essays on Christian Higher Education*. Grand Rapids: Eerdmans, 2004.

Wong, Hosanna. "Bernal Heights: Passion City Church The Grove" YouTube video, October 4, 2023. https://youtu.be/xNhvq8rZDOQ.

Yarhouse, Mark. "Understanding the Transgender Phenomenon." *Christianity Today*, June 8, 2015. https://www.christianitytoday.com/2015/06/understanding-transgender-gender-dysphoria/.

Yarhouse, Mark, and Julia Sadusky. "Best Practices in Ministry to Youth Navigating Gender Identity and Faith." *Christian Education Journal* 17 (2020) 1–12.

www.ingramcontent.com/pod-product-compliance
Lightning Source LLC
Chambersburg PA
CBHW030858170426
43193CB00009BA/655